Hey Dude, Don't *Die!*

Spanky's Ultimate Guide to Safe Driving

Chris Medina

Copyright © 2023 by Chris Medina

All rights reserved. No part of this publication may be reproduced, distributed, or transmitted in any form or by any means, including photocopying, recording, or other electronic or mechanical methods, without the prior written permission of the publisher, except in the case of brief quotations embodied in critical reviews and certain other noncommercial uses permitted by copyright law. For permission requests, email: spankysdrivingacademy@gmail.com

Page Design and Additional Cover Design: Brian Kannard

Editing: Ashley Hagan @ inkwellwriters.com

Paperback ISBN: 9798988625704
eBook ISBN: 9798988625711

Printed in the United States

1 2 3 4 5 6 7 8 9 10

This book is dedicated to all the families and friends who have lost a loved one in a traffic crash. I hope this book helps to save lives in the future.

Contents

Foreword	9
1. Active vs. Passive Driving	12
2. Aggressive Driving	17
3. Airbags	22
4. Animals	26
5. Auto Club	29
6. Bad Weather	32
7. Bicycles	36
8. Breakdowns	39
9. Buying or Leasing a Vehicle	43
10. Confidence	47
11. Construction Zones	50
12. Crashes	53
13. Crosswalks	56
14. Dashboard	59
15. Defensive Driving	63
16. Distracted Driving	66

17. DMV	69
18. Driver's Education	72
19. Drowsy Driving	75
20. Dying	78
21. Emergency Vehicles	83
22. Eye Movement	85
23. Freeways/Interstate	87
24. Fun	91
25. Funerals	94
26. Getting into the Car	99
27. Impaired Driving	102
28. Insurance	107
29. Intersections	110
30. Kindness	113
31. Lane Changes	115
32. Lane Control	118
33. License Test—The BIG day!	121
34. Maintaining Your Vehicle	124
35. Motorcycles	127
36. Night Driving	132
37. Parents	135
38. Parking Lots	139
39. Passengers	142
40. Passing	146
41. Pedestrians	149
42. Permit Test	153
43. Relationships	156
44. Right-of-Way	159

45. Road Rage	161
46. Road Trips	166
47. School Buses	169
48. School Zones	172
49. Seat Belts	174
50. Signs and Lines	178
51. Speeding	181
52. Stupidity	186
53. Traffic Court	188
54. Traffic Lights	191
55. Trains	194
56. Trust	198
57. Turning	201
Acknowledgements	205
Resources	207

Foreword

It's hard to believe that in the fall of 1982, I was sitting in my own Driver's Education class with my junior varsity football teammates. WOW! Time flies! Where have the years gone? Our teacher was Coach Martin, who also ran the track program. Sure enough, I goofed around, talked a lot, didn't pay attention, was called a hamburger by Coach Martin a couple of times, and left the semester with a C on my report card. That's right; an entire semester of Driver's Education, and my final grade was a C. Talk about a boring class! It wasn't Coach Martin's fault. I just didn't have the attention span for it. After the classroom portion was over, all the guys crammed into the car and took turns driving with Coach. I, for some reason, didn't do the driving portion. I never got a permit or a license, and I continued to get rides from Glenn, Dann, Jacquie or Bill. When it was warm, I rode my bike to school until my senior year when I bought my buddy John's yellow moped for a mere twenty dollars.

After high school I borrowed cars from friends, even though I still had no license. That was stupid! Finally, at nineteen years old, I borrowed my friend Mindi's car and drove illegally to the DMV, passed my license test, and was finally legal! Summer of '87, baby! Later that day I bought my buddy Sean's white 1967 Plymouth Fury Sport Convertible for the deal of the century of $300. How could I pass that up? That night I got my first ticket. It was called a fix-it ticket because of the terrible condition of the car. Broken brake lights, expired registration, only one headlight working, burnt out turn signal. The cop gave me a month to fix everything and bring the car and the checklist back to the station as proof, which I did.

That summer day started my actual driving career, and what a stupid way to start out. I was such a bonehead! I simply didn't care. I just kept the car between the lines and drove. I was a typical valley dude from Woodland Hills, California, enjoying the beach and the freedom of having a car.

Over the years, I racked up some speeding tickets and did my stint in a few traffic school classes, thinking how stupid and expensive they were, until my last ticket in 2000. I finally had to look in the mirror and have a chat with myself. At 32 years old, it was time for a change.

Eventually I got married, had three daughters, and started to develop a conviction to be the safest driver possible. I even resented other drivers who reminded me of my younger self. That's when a grown up starts to realize they are growing up—when they start to care about people other than themselves. A couple of years later, I randomly fell into the wacky world of Driver's Education and was hooked. Eventually I opened my own driving school called Spanky's Driving Academy. Funny name, but one you can't forget! After twenty years in the industry, I'm still alive. That's a huge victory!

While this book talks about driving in America, the principles in it are for drivers all over the world. I consider this an international book. A labor of love for all! Everyone, from everywhere, of any age can learn and apply many of these chapters to their lives. I tried to be comprehensive, and I'm sorry if I missed a topic you wanted to read and learn about, but perhaps I'll cover it down the road in another book. Applying this book to your driving life will help you become a good, safe, defensive driver and will reduce the chances of you getting into a crash, injuring yourself, injuring others, or dying. Whip out your highlighter and mark it up if needed. Let's go!

1
Active vs. Passive Driving

Now this is going to sound like a head full of freakiness, but read carefully: defensive driving is the foundation of driving. It basically means looking out for other drivers and expecting them to do the wrong thing. Active driving is also part of that foundation because it's what helps you to drive defensively. They go together, but you'll read more about defensive driving a few chapters from now.

Passive driving is lazy driving. Most people get comfortable and "settle in" to driving when they feel like they are experienced drivers. Their confidence leads them to believe they won't be the one to get into a traffic crash. You can tell by glancing over and seeing their hand positions, how their posture is and what has their attention. I've seen drivers with only one hand on the wheel or steering with their knee or thigh. I've also seen drivers with a foot up on the seat with their knee up near their chest. While it's important to be comfortable when driving, you don't want your comfortability to affect HOW you drive.

Many drivers become passive after having their license for a while. They become too relaxed in their driving skills and don't notice their change in driving habits. Many drivers become passive after traveling the same roads every day. They know every curve, every pothole and expect the same traffic patterns. That's when drivers can become vulnerable.

In my early twenties, I was addicted to french fries. I would go to a drive-thru fast-food place at least four times a week to get a large order of crispy golden fries and munch on them while driving my five-speed stick shift sports car around the streets of the San Fernando Valley in California. What a dork! I felt confident and comfortable behind the wheel, so I didn't think twice about eating while driving. I was a pretty good defensive driver, but my mind wasn't always tuned into the task at hand.

Having a license is a privilege, not a right, but I didn't fully understand that. I was in my own little world back then, and today I'm still surprised that I never caused a car crash. Because of my passive attitude toward driving, I had a couple close calls and forced other motorists to drive defensively around me.

Story Time

As I mentioned in the Foreword, I own a company called Spanky's Driving Academy. We teach Driver's Education to teens. Recently I had a driving lesson with a cool 15-year-old named Logan who had just finished the classroom portion and was now starting his behind-the-wheel lessons. Logan had his driver's permit for about six months and had been practicing a lot with his parents. He is an engaged driver and scans the road left to right pretty well. One thing Logan did that 98 percent of our teen drivers don't do is identify potholes in the road. On our first driving lesson, Logan made a left turn and within 100 feet of finishing the turn we encountered at least five potholes in the same area of the lane. Since Logan was driving actively, he was able to see the potholes quickly enough and change lanes safely to maneuver around them. I told him I was impressed and that I would mention him in this chapter. Hi Logan! Great job, dude! Thanks for not messing up the front axle or alignment on the Spanky-mobile. You saved the car. You're my hero!

Since driving a car requires multitasking, being an active driver can help decrease the chances of encountering surprise situations—like potholes!

Signs of active driving

1. Eyes scanning the road left to right, checking the rearview mirror, and looking down the road to eliminate any surprises
2. Both hands on the wheel at 9 o'clock and 3 o'clock
3. Obeying the speed limit
4. Creating enough space behind the vehicle ahead
5. Using blinkers when needed
6. Awareness of red light changing to green and being ready to go
7. Looking ahead a couple of cars to see what they do

Signs of passive driving

1. Not scanning the road
2. One hand on the wheel or even steering with the knee
3. Way below or way above the speed limit without being aware
4. Tailgating and not realizing it
5. Turning head continuously to speak with passengers
6. Having food, drink, etc., in your hand even though you have your eyes on the road
7. Elbow on the window sill with left hand on your cheek

Some of these passive driving points can turn into distracted driving, so be very careful. No matter where you're at in your driving career—new driver or driver with many years of experience—you can still make improvements. It starts with your mind. Staying focused and in the moment, being intentional and thinking ahead about lane changes, turns, and exit lanes—and being prepared for them—are a few good ways of being a more active driver.

I like to run on dirt trails in the hills, and it takes a lot of my concentration. I have to be an active runner and look down the trails and watch out to avoid divots, rocks and roots. It takes a lot of practice. A couple of times when I've been passive and not keeping my mind on the trail, I've fallen and eaten dirt. That's when I'm reminded to be an active trail runner and be engaged in what I'm doing. When driving, make sure to practice the bullet points above, and you'll see a clear difference in your awareness.

In the big picture, life should not be lived passively. Active and aware people get things done. Active and aware people understand what is going on around them. In my experience as a professional driving coach, I've noticed that teens who have an active personal life have been the better drivers. Many teens who are passive in their personal lives, who just sit around watching screens or sleeping in too late without any outside interests, tend to be the same way when they get in the car for a driving lesson. They are passive with their eye movement, lazy about their lane control, and don't apply the tools I've given them. After a couple of lessons with me, they begin to change. Amen!

So ask yourself: what kind of person are you, and what kind of person do you want to be? I hope you'll be engaged and intentional, in life and as a driver. Keep your eyes moving, process all you see so you can respond safely, and you'll do great. Someone might thank you for looking out for them. We need more heroes on the road, and active driving is one way to become that hero.

2
Aggressive Driving

Aggressive driving can be a hard habit to break, so as a new driver, you really want to get aggressive driving under control before it controls you.

Signs of an aggressive driver:

1. Speeding.
2. Weaving in and out of traffic without signaling.
3. Tailgating other vehicles.
4. Running stop signs.
5. Blocking traffic and not letting other drivers into your lane.
6. Forcing your way into other lanes.

I know about all the points above because I was THAT guy driving on the L.A. streets and freeways. I can't believe I was never in a car crash. Perhaps other drivers were looking out for me. I definitely wasn't looking out for them. Come on! I had places to go, people to see and fun to have! I couldn't be slowed down by traffic or idiot drivers. Oh, so you're saying I was the idiot driver? You are correct!

So why do people drive aggressively? Most of the time it's because they know they can get away with it. You'll notice people obey the law when there's a cop around, but when the cops are nowhere to be found, drivers do what they want. Another reason people drive aggressively is because they don't manage their time well and always rush to get places. At Spanky's, we also teach a traffic school class for drivers who got a ticket. Many of those students tell me they like to speed and weave in and out of traffic because they are naturally impatient people. But when impatience leads to aggressive driving, it can be deadly. Most people are emotional drivers, not logical drivers, and many drivers lose their cool and morph into hotheaded idiots if something happens they don't like. Driving does something to people, and there are a ton of studies on the psychology of driving for you to check out online sometime.

What happens if you drive aggressively?

1. You could get into a car crash, be injured, or die.
2. You could cause a car crash with injuries or death.
3. You could get a ticket and lose time and money.
4. You could have your license suspended or revoked.

Story Time

I was coming back from a great weekend in the mountains. I had been at a church camp, and I was driving the church van with a dozen teens inside. We were on the freeway in southern California when I saw a sports car flying up from behind us. I thought he was going to rear-end us, but instead, he switched lanes and blew past us on the left. He then drove about a quarter of a mile ahead of us and tried to pass a car on the right, where slower traffic was. The driver hit a trailer being towed by a Jeep, and pieces of the trailer flew everywhere into the sky. It was demolished. The Jeep was a mess as well and tipped over on its side. I quickly pulled the church van over onto the shoulder, as traffic was now completely stopped. I told the teens to stay in the van as I got out to check for injuries. The speeder had gotten out of his crunched car and started to flee the scene of the crash by running under the wire fence off the freeway. I chased him down and caught him very quickly and stayed with him for a few minutes until police arrived. The police called me a few days later and told me the driver of the Jeep had died. I was crushed to hear that news. That aggressive driver's impatience caused him to speed and pass vehicles on the right where slower traffic was, and the result was that he killed someone.

Another Story

One of our traffic school students named Mark got pulled over and given a huge ticket for aggressive driving because he was tailgating and weaving in and out of traffic. He reached a speed of 125 miles per hour. The judge put him on a six-month probation, with two weeks of community service. Mark said his car was in the shop and he borrowed his mom's Corvette and didn't realize he was going that fast. The entire class laughed at him. He laughed, too. I didn't. I had already seen what happens when people drive aggressively.

A few tips for dealing with aggressive drivers:

1. Don't get involved. If you are being tailgated, move a lane to your right and get them out of your life. If there is no lane to move to, then perhaps turn right at the next parking lot or corner. It may take 30 seconds out of your life, but at least the tailgater is gone.

2. Don't brake-check other vehicles. Feel free to throw out your left hand and wave them around you if you're going slower than they want to go. Perhaps they'll go around you when it's safe and legal. Perhaps they'll go around you illegally, but stay calm and let them do their thing and move on. Be nice!

3. Don't take their driving personally. You don't know each other. They are in their own selfish little world. Don't let their driving affect the way you drive. Sometimes drivers will be extra bold and may even try to intimidate you. Just be careful, don't get emotional or involve your ego, or you could find yourself in a situation that you might regret. Be the hero.

A few tips to keep you from becoming an aggressive driver:

1. Leave early for your destination so you don't stress yourself out and change your driving behavior.
2. Get plenty of rest so you are not irritable and take it out on other drivers.
3. Count to ten and say to yourself, "It ain't worth it."
4. At the start of your drive, determine that you are going to be the hero on the road that day.

If you start your day with a deliberate attitude of being the hero and caring about other drivers, you'll decrease your chances of losing your self-control. Just chill out and be cool!

3
Airbags

Have you ever been punched in the face? It hurts, right? Imagine being hit in the face by an airbag coming at you at twice the speed of a baseball pitcher's fastball! OUCH! Even though it's a safety measure, airbags have the potential to harm you as well. The steering wheel airbag can deploy as fast as 200 miles per hour, or about 1/25 of a second. So if it hits you in the face, it can hurt...A LOT! Airbags are generally made of nylon, and they're inflated with either nitrogen or argon gas. Once the airbag deploys, it needs to immediately deflate or else your face ends up hitting it when it's as hard as a rock. When it deflates, it gives your body's momentum a chance to slow down.

It's crazy to think that the idea for airbags was thought of as far back as 1919 when two dentists filed a patent. Over the next few decades, different men tinkered with their inventions and filed different patents for airbags, but it was in the 1970's that they started to gain attention as a safety device. Finally, in the late 1980's, they caught on big time and grew in popularity. Since the late 1990's, airbags have been required in all vehicles, and since then they've saved over 50,000 lives in the United States alone.

When you get into a crash, sensors in your vehicle deploy the airbags, and they help to save you from injury or death by protecting you from hitting the steering wheel, dashboard, or windshield. Today there can be as many as ten airbags in just one car! They are strategically placed all over the vehicle, from side airbags in the door to steering wheel and dashboard airbags in front of the driver to airbags that are overhead in the ceiling. Airbags working with seat belts AND defensive driving are the safest you can get.

Story Time

One of those long extension ladders fell off a truck on the freeway in Los Angeles. A bunch of drivers slammed on their brakes really hard and created a big mess. Many cars got rear-ended, and some airbags went off. I heard the collisions very loudly from the overpass above, where I was walking back to my car after a lunch appointment. I managed to climb down an embankment and approached a cargo van to see if I could help. The driver was slumped over his steering wheel. I checked his pulse and confirmed he was alive. He had been knocked unconscious by the airbag! I then took out my new 1998 mobile cellular device (cell phone) and called the phone number painted on the side of his truck to let them know that Steve (the name on his shirt) would not be coming back to the office that afternoon. I waited with Steve for a few minutes until first responders arrived. Steve regained consciousness a minute or two later but had no idea what had happened.

That's what happens when you are too close to the airbag during a crash. Airbags help reduce the risk of injury or death, but you need to stay out of their way, because they can hurt you pretty bad, and then you're walking around for five or six days with red airbag burn on your face. I've seen it. It looks weird. Especially if it hits half your face. Keep your hands at 9 o'clock and 3 o'clock on the steering wheel so the airbag doesn't knock your hands up to your face, especially if you have long nails or are wearing a watch, rings, or bracelets. You don't want to be walking around looking like Franken-babe or Franken-dude with stitches and scars all over your face. Who's going to want to go to the prom with you? I'm serious.

A few tips for staying safe when your airbag deploys:

1. Keep your butt on your seat and feet on the floor. That will allow the airbag to work correctly with your body position, which reduces the possibility of injury.

2. If you are the driver, keep your hands at 9 o'clock and 3 o'clock on the steering wheel and stay ten to twelve inches away so it has a chance to deploy and deflate without hitting you in your gorgeous face.

3. If you are the passenger in the front seat, never put your feet up on the dashboard while the car is in motion. If there is a crash, it could violently throw your knees up to your face, and you could lose a bunch of teeth.

4. Don't drive with pets on your lap. Think about that visual. There could be dog parts all over you, plus you could be injured as well.

More Good Than Harm

In one year back in the early days of passenger dashboard airbags, nine infants were killed by the airbag because they were in their infant seats in the front seat. After that, the law was changed so that infants have to be seated in the back seat in a rear-facing child car seat until they are at least one year old and twenty pounds. Amen on that!

The good news is that statistics prove airbags do more good than harm. The National Highway Transportation Safety Administration (NHTSA) reported that in one year alone, airbags reduced the chance of dying in a frontal crash by 61 percent. That's huge! And between the years 1987-2017, frontal airbags saved 50,457 lives. That's huge too!

I can go on and on about airbags, but do yourself a favor and read more about them online. I think you'll actually be fascinated by all the studies and hard work that smart people put into the airbag industry. You can even watch airbag videos. You'll end up knowing more about them than the average person, and everyone will think you are really smart!

4
Animals

If you're like me, then you love animals. I've had dogs, cats, hamsters and birds. They are fun and provide joy to me. Except when they poop! But that's no reason to run over them—so don't. The problem is they are hard to avoid sometimes because we have so many animals running into the streets and onto the highways. That's why it is important that you keep scanning from left to right to give yourself a chance to brake in time if an animal darts out in front of you. At the same time, you have to glance in your rearview mirror to see how close the vehicles are behind you because you don't want to get rear-ended if you have to suddenly slam on your brakes.

If you hit a domestic pet like a dog or cat, then try to find the owner. Also, don't jerk the wheel to the left and go into oncoming traffic to avoid hitting an animal. That decision could change a lot of lives. You could hit a mom with kids in the car or perhaps hit a giant cement truck. Unfortunately, it's sometimes best to continue driving and run over a little critter if it would be more dangerous to swerve out of the way.

Story Time

A dad was driving along a dark, two-lane highway at night with his four kids in the car. Dad was driving at the speed limit when a huge deer came onto the road and jumped at the car, attempting to jump over it. The deer went through the windshield and injured all the family members. His 8-year-old daughter died from her injuries.

The dad wasn't at fault, and there was probably nothing he could have done differently, but stories like this one should motivate us to be extra cautious on back roads at night. The dad might have driven that same road countless times and felt comfortable that night. Anything can happen at any time, so it's important to keep scanning left to right, especially at night, to avoid hitting animals while driving.

Another Story

I was being tailgated once at about 9:00 at night. I was 800 feet from my driveway, going about 30 miles per hour, when a cute little bunny hopped out in front of me. I was about to slam my brakes on but couldn't for fear of being rear-ended and injured. I had to keep going, and sure enough, I hit little Bruno the bunny and POOF—white bunny fur flew everywhere in front of my headlights. I was so angry at the tailgater for not allowing me to brake harder. It almost sent me to therapy!

A few tips to help you avoid animals:

1. Scan the road left to right.
2. Use your high beams when needed.
3. Glance in the rearview mirror every five seconds so you know how close vehicles are behind you.
4. Don't tailgate other drivers because if they swerve to avoid an animal, you have a better chance of also seeing it in time to avoid hitting it yourself.
5. Don't swerve into oncoming traffic to avoid an animal. Something worse can happen.

    I know this isn't a topic we like to discuss, but it's a matter of life and death, so it's important to address. Lastly, if you hit a squirrel or bunny and bring it home to put in your evening soup, then that's up to you. I won't judge you. But dude, that's gross!

5
Auto Club

I personally believe that everyone needs to become a member of an auto club. I belong to AAA (Automobile Association of America). It's an organization I highly promote. I've benefitted greatly by paying an inexpensive yearly membership for their services. Each year I am able to call them four times when something goes wrong with my vehicle.

Some things AAA has helped me with:

1. A dead battery
2. When I locked my keys in my truck
3. When my truck didn't start and needed to be towed

If you are a member and you're with a non-member when their vehicle breaks down, you can call AAA, and they will come out to help. That's awesome!

There are other auto clubs out there, so do your research to see which one works best for you. One tow per year can cost double than what the membership costs annually, so it is wise to join one.

Story Time

One cold, snowy night when I was teaching in Minnesota, a mom came to pick her daughter up after class and discovered her minivan's tire was flat. I offered to put on her spare tire but had a lot of trouble trying to release the spare tire stored under the vehicle. My hands were freezing, and the lock bolt on the spare tire was on too tight. That's when I realized I was able to call AAA and have someone come out to fix the flat. Within an hour, a really cool AAA dude drove up and fixed the flat within 30 minutes. The mom tipped him ten dollars, and he was very grateful. He told her she was the first person to tip him during his long, cold ten-hour shift. So make sure you give them a tip if you can as a way of showing your appreciation. It will go a long way.

Another time I was in the car ready to leave for work and realized I left my sunglasses in the house. As usual, when I got out of the car, I locked the door. But this time I had the keys in the ignition. Bad move! As the car door was closing, I lunged back as fast as I could to keep it from closing but it was too late. I had locked the keys in the ignition WITH the car turned on and engine running. What a bonehead. No worries! I called AAA, and they arrived within an hour. The guy worked his magic with a slim rod and unlocked my car within 20 seconds. I tipped him lunch money for a burger. He was grateful and I was EXTRA grateful and was able to get to a driving lesson on time.

Other Ways to Save Money

While some breakdowns are unavoidable, we can all do our part to lessen the chances of automobile issues that frustrate us and dent our wallet. We'll talk more about maintenance in a future chapter, but maintaining your vehicle could keep you from having to call your auto club for help.

A few tips to avoid a call to the auto club:

1. Take your time and know where your keys are at all times. And have spare keys.
2. Check your tires often to see how worn they are. Make sure your spare tire is inflated.
3. Check oil and fluid levels often. You can even stop by your oil change place and have them top off your fluids, if needed. They usually do it for free.

It can save you a lot of extra headaches being part of an auto club with an affordable annual membership. It would have cost me more having the locksmith come out just one time than having the membership for four "calls." So join an auto club and keep their card in your wallet or glove compartment.

6
Bad Weather

I can't believe I'm still alive after all these years of driving in bad weather with teens. Most of the time I'm pretty chill since I have about twenty years of driving coaching under my belt, but on a rare occasion, my nerves get tested. It's hard for me to think of myself as a professional driving coach (instructor), but it's nights like the other night, when I drove with a teen girl who had about five hours of driving experience but none at night in the rain, that I'm reminded. When I get a teen to settle down, read the weather and road conditions correctly, understand the situation, and drive accordingly, I realize that parents really do trust me (the professional) and need me to get them and their teen through the "pain cave" of driving.

It's important to get in as much drive time as you can with your parents during the winter months before you get your license because you'll need that experience come the following winter when you are driving by yourself. Most parents do not want to take their teen out to practice driving in bad weather conditions. But how is a teen going to get the experience of driving in bad conditions if their parents avoid it? Parents, I know it can be scary, because I had three teen drivers of my own, but teens need to experience driving in bad weather as much as possible before they're driving independently, or the chances of them getting in a crash go up a ton.

Story Time

One spring day, I was driving with a teen in the light rain when the DJ on the radio confirmed what we had known about all morning—we had tornado conditions coming. The teen slowed down and kept her distance from the cars in front of her. One thing many drivers don't do in light rain is change their driving habits. They think they can handle the light rain but don't realize that hydroplaning (sliding on a thin layer of water) can still happen. Being from California, I was used to some rain and the occasional earthquake, but not tornados. I'm not really into destruction. I didn't feel like getting sucked up at 400 miles per hour and thrown into a field eight miles away. It was weird watching the sky change color to a kind of greenish tint with dark clouds. As the sky changed its tone, I noticed other drivers started driving faster to get where they needed to go, which is what you don't want to do. We drove back to her house safely and ended the lesson about ten minutes early so I could get back on the freeway to get to my own house. As I was driving, the rain got heavier by the minute.

Fortunately, no tornados touched the ground, but I was still pretty nervous.

A few tips when driving in bad weather:

1. Don't drive if you don't have to.
2. Be flexible. Change plans to another day.
3. Buckle up and go slow.
4. Make a plan. Think of easier routes to get to your destination.
5. Leave early enough to reach your destination on time.
6. Leave plenty of room in front and on both sides of your vehicle.
7. Use your low beams in foggy weather.
8. Pull well off the road and wait a while if the weather takes an extra turn for the worse.
9. Try to find weather reports on the radio.
10. Have your speed match the weather and road conditions. Use wisdom.

When it's drizzling out, you must change your driving behavior. If it hasn't rained in a couple of weeks, the residue of thousands of vehicles' worth of dripped transmission fluid, oil, and other fluids will mix with the first light rain and create slippery areas on the road. I've often noticed hearing fire trucks near my office when it first begins to rain, which tells me people have been hydroplaning on the slick roads. Cars can easily slide on wet roads as it is, but when it first begins to rain, the roads are extra slippery.

Most bridges are made out of steel or iron and tend to freeze before regular roads, so be very careful when crossing a bridge in the winter. Even in the South, most areas have salt trucks that drop salt to melt ice and snow on main roads, but many back roads don't get salted, so be extra careful on those. Also, watch out for potholes and divots in the road. They can pop your tires if it's extremely cold out. I've seen it happen.

The best advice I can give you is to check the weather and plan ahead. Be flexible and be willing to change your plans to work around the weather. Better to be safe than sorry.

7
Bicycles

Bikes are a great way to get around. They don't require gas, and they are great exercise. As a kid, I rode my bike everywhere. It was often one hundred degrees in the hot San Fernando Valley during the summers, so I thrived on riding down the hills and coasting in the hot wind to the store to get my candy bar and soda. Back in the late 70's and early 80's, I pretty much went everywhere on my bike. My bike meant freedom to me. I rode on the sidewalks a lot, and then would jump off the curb into the street. I would even race my friends down the street. We were honked at by cars and we freaked out a lot of drivers. I used to ride my bike to school with a bunch of neighborhood kids. We would ride through stop signs and not obey the cross walks. It's a wonder I made it to twelfth grade!

When driving a car, however, you have to remember that the bike riders also have the same rights to the road as we do, except that obviously they aren't allowed on freeways. We have to share the road with them and always keep our eyes scanning for them. Most bike riders stay on the right side of the road and obey all the same traffic laws as vehicles.

The problem is that many bike riders can be unpredictable. I've seen some of the hardcore bike riders with their tights on and logos splattered on their shirts fly down the road too far out from the shoulder. It's tough to get around them. When sharing the road with a bike rider, be prepared for them to make sudden moves. Perhaps they move to the left to avoid a pothole in the road, pieces of tire, or other types of debris. I've also seen more bike riders wearing ear buds and listening to music while riding, and that can be deadly.

In this day and age, we now have to share the road with electric bikes as well. They have batteries you can plug in and charge, and they even move faster than your average kid on his ten-speed. Some electric bikes can go as fast as 28 miles per hour.

Story Time

A dad who was training for one of his many triathlons was on his bike doing his thing when he was struck by a car. The driver wasn't paying attention and sent the dad flying. He died of a head injury even while wearing a helmet. Yes, it can happen. He left behind three kids and a wonderful wife.

Another person was riding his bike when a car passed him up on the left and then cut the biker off when making a right turn in front of him. The biker hit the car and fell off. While there were no broken bones, the guy was scraped up and pretty sore for a few days.

A few tips for driving when bikes are present:

1. Scan the road left to right and as far ahead as possible.
2. If you see a bike rider on your right and you want to pass him, make sure to give him at least three feet of space.
3. Don't pull the "right hook" on a bike rider. That's making a right turn in front of him. He will probably hit your vehicle.
4. Don't pull the "left hook" on a bike rider as well. That's making a left turn in front of the bike rider who's coming straight toward you through an intersection.
5. Watch out that you don't T-bone a bike rider coming from your left or right. Many bike riders run stop signs in residential areas.

According to the Centers for Disease Control and Prevention, there are almost 1,000 bicyclist deaths and over 130,000 injuries each year on the roads. It's very important that you put the distractions aside and drive intentionally with your eyes constantly moving. One day you might see a teen riding their bike the way I used to, so you really want to be prepared. You don't want to be involved in any type of car-bike crash whatsoever.

8
Breakdowns

Having your vehicle break down on you WHILE driving can be a mind freak of an experience. Breakdowns can happen anywhere at any time. They come in all sorts of frustration levels. I know because I've been there. I've rated them on a scale of 1-10 based on my own frustration level, inconvenience, time and expense. Here are some of them:

1. Flat tire: 5 out of 10 because I know how to fix a flat tire, but it might be freezing out or hot out. It won't be too expensive to replace a tire. Learning to fix a flat is a great skill to learn.

2. Radiator overheats: 7 out of 10 because you'll have to wait for a while for the radiator to cool off and then find some water or antifreeze to put in it in order to get it to a mechanic to get checked out. The radiator

might need to be replaced, and that will cost more than a tire.

3. Dead battery: 4 out of 10. You can call AAA and they'll bring you a new battery and swap it out for you, and you can pay them on the spot. Or you can always find someone to jump start your vehicle if one of you has jumper cables. Always have jumper cables.

4. Car doesn't start at all: 8 out of 10. For me, it's the fear of the unknown. If the service engine light isn't on, it could be any number of things, from the starter to the alternator. If the service engine light goes on, then take it to a mechanic as soon as you can and pray it's not the transmission. Replacing a transmission will cost BIG bucks!

Story Time

I was driving my Mitsubishi Eclipse 5-speed stick shift home from work at about 9:00 pm. I was wearing a shirt and tie and was tired at the end of a long day. I was in the left lane (fast lane), when suddenly the car lost all power. It completely stopped working. I almost started to freak out. I had never experienced a vehicle just STOP working WHILE driving.

Fortunately, my brain told me not to panic; I put the car in neutral and turned on the hazard lights to warn other drivers I had an emergency. I moved over to the right a couple of lanes and exited down the off-ramp. I did the best I could NOT to apply the brakes too much because I didn't have any power to the car and didn't want to lose momentum. If I applied my brakes too much, I would be going too slow for traffic, and that could add more danger to the situation.

As I came down the off-ramp, I prayed for a green light so I could make a smooth left turn and then pull over. I didn't want to be on the shoulder of the freeway at night, which can be very dangerous, as you can imagine. If the light had been red, then I would have simply pulled onto the shoulder of the off-ramp near the bottom. Well, the light was green, and I was able to make a normal left turn, pull over, and park next to the curb. I tried starting the engine multiple times with no luck. Fortunately, I was only about two miles from home, and I remembered that I had rollerblades in my backseat. I took off my nice shoes and skated home in my shirt and tie. I was glad it was a nice, spring evening and not raining out!

The next day I had the car towed to a mechanic, and he determined it was a bad alternator that drained the battery and stopped the car from working. A few hundred dollars later, I was back on the road. I may not have done everything correctly that night, but I'm glad it all worked out. The big thing is that I tried to keep my composure out there and not lose my cool. It's very important to have a plan of action for yourself when driving.

These days, I don't even drive in the far left lane. I like the right lane now because I have quick access to the shoulder or the nearest off-ramp.

A few tips in case of a breakdown on city streets or the freeway:

1. Turn hazard lights on immediately.

2. Take a deep breath.//
3. Check your blind spots and mirrors as you slow down to move toward the right shoulder. Moving to a left side shoulder (if there is one) can be too dangerous because of faster traffic.
4. Move as far to the right as possible on that shoulder because people not only steer with their hands, they steer with their eyes and can drive way too close to you.
5. Phone for help as soon as possible.
6. Stay with your vehicle—don't go wandering off from the car because you might be too difficult to see.
7. Raise your hood and put out cones or reflectors if you have them. But be careful!

It's common to be afraid of breaking down somewhere, so it's important that you know what to do if it happens. That way you are prepared. You can also look online for more tips to help yourself. Treat your car like a pet you love because it's what's getting you around on a daily basis. Don't take it for granted, and take good care of it!

9
Buying or Leasing a Vehicle

Buying my first car from my buddy Sean when I was 19 years old was such a great feeling. I had more freedom and could go where I wanted and when I wanted. I bet it will be the same awesome feeling for you. Perhaps right now you're driving your parents' car, and that's perfectly fine. You might not be in the position to afford your own car. Sean's car was the old 1967 convertible I mentioned earlier, and it was a good "starter" car for me. I didn't make much money back then. As I got older, made a higher income, and developed good credit, I was introduced to the crazy world of leasing a car. Leasing a vehicle gave me the opportunity to drive a brand new vehicle without the worries of breaking down or needing a lot of upkeep. Whether you buy a car or lease one depends on what your needs are.

Buying a Car

When you buy a car, you either pay the price for the car upfront in full (which means you own the title), or you can get an auto loan and pay it off over time with interest. The car dealer or the bank will ask for a down payment (a percentage of the price) upfront, and then you will make monthly payments until the loan is paid off. When you make your final payment, you will receive the title for the car (you will own it). With a loan, you will pay more money over time than if you paid for the car in full, but many people don't have the cash set aside to do that, and a monthly payment fits their budget better. Whether you own the title immediately or are making payments, it is your responsibility to pay for any maintenance or breakdowns. Which is why car insurance is important!

Leasing a Car

Leasing is essentially renting a car for a certain amount of time. When you lease a vehicle, you will have to give it back at the end of the term. At that point you are given the option to buy it at a pre-determined amount or lease another vehicle. Most lease agreements are three-year terms, and the car dealership requires a down payment unless you have stellar credit. The dealership will take care of all major repairs that arise during the term, but it's still up to you to take care of regular maintenance things, like oil changes, brake replacements, and tire rotations, unless you include those as part of your contract. Usually you have to agree to drive no more than 36,000 miles during the three years, or you will be charged ten cents per mile over the mileage. So if you drive 10,000 extra miles, you'll owe them $1,000, and that will be due at the end of the lease. That's what happened to me when I leased a brand new Toyota Camry with no miles on it. I loved that Camry and had a blast driving it for three years. Instead of having to pay back $1,000 for the mileage overage, they added the $1,000 into the overall payments on my next lease. It turned out to be about $30 extra per month for the next three years. Such is life when you are in the wacky world of leasing.

Leasing might be a good option for some because the dealer takes care of most repairs, which means you don't have to. But it also means that at the end of the lease, you don't own the car. For me, after leasing cars for six years, I realized that had I bought a car instead of leasing, I would have owned it after four years. Instead, at the end of six years, I had paid a lot of money each month only to have to turn the car back in at the end of the term.

Story Time

A few years ago, I bought a used Ford Expedition with a monthly payment, paid it off, and owned it outright after four years. It had a lot of miles on it. Unfortunately, after about five months with no payments, the transmission had issues. Just my luck. But we were able to sell it and use that money as a down payment on another used Ford Expedition. We paid off the second Expedition and enjoyed a few months of no payments before that one also developed a transmission issue. Oh well! That's what happens when you own a vehicle. It gets older, goes down in value, and sometimes you'll have to band-aid it by throwing money at it every few months. Will it still cost less overall than having a lease payment every month?

You'll have to make that determination for yourself. The big wish for most owners is to own a car that is paid off and still in amazing shape that will keep running for years and years with minimal issues. Do your research. Whip out your calculator to run your numbers, and see what is best for your budget and your peace of mind.

A few things to think about when buying or leasing a car:

1. Do I want a car payment for years and years?
2. Will I drive a lot of miles over the next few years?
3. How much down payment is needed, if any?
4. What are the pros vs. cons of buying or leasing?
5. What is the interest rate if I need a loan?

You'll need to do a lot of research to determine which is the best route for you. You'll have to figure out your budget and make a plan so you can be happy with the outcome. Ask your friends and family what they did, and perhaps one of them can refer you to a trusted car dealership. Protect your money so you don't give it away in a debt you'll regret.

10
Confidence

One of the biggest jobs I have as a driving coach is helping young people with their confidence. Confidence is pretty much the driving force behind the growth of a new driver. I've worked with teens who have straight A's in school who have no confidence in their driving, and I've worked with teens who don't do very well in school who feel very comfortable and confident behind the wheel. The one thing they all have in common is that they can't fake being a good driver. Driving ability comes with driving availability: the more time and miles you practice on the road, the more you'll improve. Without confidence, you can be a dangerous driver. An indecisive driver with a lack of confidence could make last-second decisions that would cause a crash.

Driving is both mental and emotional at the same time. It's personal; when you get something as dangerous as cars moving at high speeds, emotions will be involved. We've had teens in our program whose fear keeps them from wanting to drive. Fear is also what gets in the way of parents wanting to drive with their teens. That can cause anxiety in the teen driver, and he or she may go three more years without testing for their license. I've had a ton of phone calls over the years from parents of 19- and 20-year-olds wanting to take lessons because they weren't mentally ready for it in the past.

Story Time

Years ago, I had a sweet older teen named Monique call me up to join our program. She was in twelfth grade, eighteen years old, and had failed her driving test, even though she passed it. Huh? The driving examiner told her that even though she technically passed the test, she couldn't in good conscience give Monique a driver's license because she wasn't confident enough to drive by herself. The examiner believed it was too dangerous. She told Monique to take our course to gain ability and confidence. We had a great time in the classroom and also on her driving lessons. However, one day on a lesson, Monique was waiting to make a left turn into a parking lot and froze. She wasn't sure whether to stay put or finish her turn, so she made a half-turn and stopped in the lane, with traffic approaching. I told her to keep going, but she wouldn't move. It took me saying three times to go, go, go—and she finally did and got us in the parking lot. She was really shaken, so I had her park the car. That's when the tears started coming down. She didn't understand why she froze up like that. We sat there for a few minutes while she composed herself. She asked me to say a prayer for her, and I did, and then we drove some more and finished on a good note. After finishing our program, Monique retested a few weeks later and passed. I was so proud of her. She was even promoted to assistant manager at her job because she finally had a license and could travel to multiple stores.

A few tips to help your confidence:

1. Drive often and put in a bunch of miles each time.
2. Celebrate each time you get back to your house without a ticket or crash.
3. Keep reminding yourself of those successes. It will help your confidence.
4. Make sure whoever is practicing with you is keeping you encouraged.
5. Push away any negative thoughts. They have no business in your driving.

The more you drive, the more growth you'll see. Consistency is important, so pull out your calendar and make a plan to drive as much as you can each week. Practice makes progress, and progress is huge! Progress means you are better than yesterday. You can do it!

11
Construction Zones

Did you know that a worker is killed in a highway construction work zone almost every day of the year in the United States? That's well over 300 people each year! It is why many work zone fines will be doubled if you get a ticket.

Research tells us that, on average, it takes about five years for a new driver to become an "average driver." In fact, almost 50 percent of all new drivers will either get a ticket or be involved in a crash their first year of driving. Many of these crashes will be in work zones. On a weekly basis I have to tell 90 percent of our student drivers to slow down and pay extra attention in work zones. There is so much going on in those zones that it makes it difficult to process. That's why young people have to be very intentional and very careful.

Story Time

The last time I got a ticket was in 1999 while driving through a construction zone on a Sunday night in the rain with no one working. The speed limit was 60 in the work zone and was clearly marked in orange, but I chose to continue going 70 miles per hour. The fact that it was dark and raining should have kicked in a little wisdom and caused me to slow down—but I didn't.

Highway patrol pulled me over, and the officer walked up to the car to have a little chat with me. I figured he'd give me a warning rather than a ticket, considering it was pouring out and he was getting drenched. The wind was fierce, and it was practically raining sideways. I was getting pelted in the face by the rain when I was speaking with him, even with my window only rolled down a little, but the officer was determined to give me a ticket and teach me a lesson.

A few weeks later, I had to attend a four-hour traffic school class to work off the ticket while sitting under an outdoor covering with about 150 other law breakers (mostly speeders and aggressive drivers). But much to my surprise, I enjoyed the class.

I really learned the importance of slowing down and being extra aware in highway and street work zones. In fact, that was my very last ticket before I decided to look in the mirror, have a little chat with my idiot self, and change my driving behavior.

A few tips for driving in construction zones:

1. Look well ahead so there are no surprises. That will help you see any upcoming work zones ahead.
2. Work zones are usually marked very clearly with orange construction signs and occasional yellow warning signs as well.
3. When you're in a work zone, slow down and scan left to right.
4. Obey any worker who has a flag in his hand directing traffic.
5. Watch out for the orange cones and drums so you don't hit them and send them flying into other cars or a worker.

The next time you see an overpass memorialized with a person's name on it, there's a good chance that person was a highway worker killed while on the job. If you take your time, pay attention, and slow down, you'll get through those work zones with ease. If you spend your time doing the right things on the road, then you won't have the time to do the wrong things on the road. Just be cool!

12

Crashes

One of my biggest fears is the possibility of one of my daughters being in a car crash. I know they are safe drivers, but what about the drivers they are sharing the roads with? Are they safe drivers as well? Car crashes are the leading cause of death for teens. The National Safety Council (NSC) reports there are more than 4.5 million people injured each year in car crashes. That's over 12,000 injuries each day. The NSC also reported that since 2020 we've averaged over 40,000 motor vehicle crash deaths each year as well. Those numbers are scary! So what can you do to avoid a car crash? You have to move your eyes and be aware of what is going on around you, keep your concentration on your driving, and drive defensively.

Story Time

I was driving down the street one day on wet roads when a man and wife pulled out of a parking lot right in front of me and stopped. I hit my brakes, but I still slammed into them. It was minor front end damage to my bumper with no injuries. The older gentleman apologized and had his insurance pay for a new bumper. I was inconvenienced for a week because I had to take the bus around town while the car was in the shop, but the car looked great after it was repaired, and I moved on with my life.

On another night, my college roommate Kurt and I were meeting some friends for dinner when a young woman made a left turn in front of us on a yellow light. Instead of fixing his car, the other driver's insurance company cut Kurt a check for $2,000 because his car was going to cost the insurance company more than two grand to fix. The crash wasn't his fault, and yet he was totally inconvenienced for it financially. Kurt used the two grand as a down payment on a newer car and was stuck with a three-year monthly payment. Unfortunately, that's the way the world works sometimes.

If you do get into a crash, here's what you should do:

1. If there is no serious injury, then try moving vehicles to the side of the road as soon as you safely can.
2. Call the police to come take an incident report if your state law requires it. Or call them anyway.

3. Get the other driver's info: phone number, address, license number, registration information and insurance information.

4. Make sure you have your insurance card in your center console or your glove compartment. I have mine in an envelope with the registration in the glove compartment.

5. Take photos or video and perhaps record some commentary for your own memory. Let's face it, car crashes happen fast, and our memory gets foggy when some level of trauma to our thoughts and system happens. If you haven't been in a fender bender before, then you might say or do things you don't remember simply because you've never been in that situation before. I'm not talking about because of injury; it's a new negative experience. So try to stay calm and in the moment with as much clarity as possible. Don't get emotional.

In my research, I've discovered that up to 98 percent of all car crashes are human error, with a crash occurring every five seconds in this country. Let that sink into your brain. So be careful, scan the road left to right, and keep those eyes moving.

13
Crosswalks

Crosswalks are areas that pedestrians use to get from one corner of an intersection to another. They require great awareness on behalf of every driver. Many crosswalks have traffic lights that let pedestrians know when they are allowed to cross, while other crosswalks have either stop signs or nothing at all. You've probably been on the wrong end of a car versus pedestrian situation in a crosswalk, when a car stopped at the crosswalk line with his front end sticking out in your way, making you walk either behind his vehicle or in front. I always walk behind. I don't trust those drivers to be paying attention. Usually if there are two crosswalk lines, then there is a thick white stop line a few feet before the crosswalk line. Drivers should stop behind that stop line to allow plenty of space for pedestrians to use the crosswalk. If there is no stop line, then stop at the crosswalk line without going over it.

A few tips when approaching a crosswalk:

1. Slow down sooner than normal so you don't stop over the crosswalk or stop line.

2. Watch to your right because there might be parked cars close to the corner, blocking your view of pedestrians who are about to step off the curb into the crosswalk.

3. You must yield to pedestrians already in the crosswalk. Don't drive around them. You could get a "failure to yield to a pedestrian" ticket because pedestrians have the right-of-way.

4. When making a right turn on a red light, be sure to make a complete stop before the lines to obey the law, then move forward slowly to get a better look to your left, AND check across the intersection for vehicles with a left turn protected arrow. Also, be sure no pedestrians are walking up to the crosswalk because you could block them if you are sitting there too long before moving forward.

5. Remember, if your head is turned to your left too long waiting for traffic to clear before your right turn, you could have pedestrians walking in front of your vehicle in the crosswalk. So turn your head a couple of times to your right to see if kids are approaching from the sidewalk on skate boards or bikes, or Granny is walking her dog.

    I've seen drivers either not paying attention and not yielding to pedestrians, or being aggressive and "pressing" the situation by moving forward a little bit at a time to "hurry" the pedestrian into walking faster to the other side of the street. Neither of those is safe. Just be cool, drive safely, and watch out for pedestrians. The last thing people using the crosswalk need is another idiot driver ruining their day.

14
Dashboard

Dashboards can be very sophisticated these days, so it's essential that every driver know their way around the one in their car. We are now in the "new world" of hybrid and electric vehicles, and it's only going to grow and grow. Have you ever seen the inside of a car that is twenty-five years old? Imagine what the inside of a car will look like twenty-five years from now. The car world has totally changed, so help yourself and go out to Mom or Dad's car, turn on the ignition, and watch it light up like the inside of a jet plane. In recent years, all the car companies have really stepped up their game and added more options with more buttons and screens for you to see what's going on with your vehicle, so pay attention and learn what they mean.

    Read through the owner's manual of your car and learn what everything is and where it's located. You'll need to know that information on the day you test for your license. Our local driver's license examiner specifically told me to make sure our teens know where everything is located on the dashboard, especially how to turn on the lights. He's had teens fail their driving test before they even put the car in gear because they didn't even know how to turn on the lights.

Each time you drive an unfamiliar vehicle, take a minute and look over the entire dashboard so you know where things are. Different cars put things in different places. More and more cars have keyless ignition buttons and other special gizmos. Driving is multi-tasking in and of itself, so to add extra buttons or dials to the car can make for distracted driving, especially if you are unfamiliar with them. Remember this: anything that takes your eyes or your mind off the road is distracted driving. And let's face it—the dashboard can be very distracting.

Another thing to note is where the gearshift is located. That has changed over the years in many cars, as well. Sometimes the gearshift is on the column near the steering wheel, and sometimes it's next to your right leg. Recently I saw it as multiple button tabs under the radio that I simply push or pull. Crazy times we live in! Henry Ford would flip out if he saw the advancements in cars today.

If the dashboard's buttons and dials weren't enough of a distraction, there are lights and symbols that will illuminate from time to time to inform you of things going on with your vehicle. Sometimes it's just telling you it's time for an oil change, but other times it's letting you know your car needs a mechanic. So don't ignore them. The owner's manual will let you know what all of those symbols mean.

Story Time

Years ago, a student of ours was really excited to take his road test for his driver's license. He went through our entire program, completing thirty hours of classroom lessons and six hours of driving lessons. His parents worked really hard helping him get all his required miles and hours completed. The one thing they dropped the ball on was allowing him to take the driving test with his mom's new minivan, which Josh had rarely driven. When the test examiner attempted to go over the dashboard with Josh, he didn't know how to turn on the lights or where the windshield wipers were. He got flustered and it all went downhill from there. Unfortunately, the examiner failed him before they even hit the road. That was a huge bummer for him! Josh had to make another appointment to take the test again a couple weeks later, and he passed with no errors. So take your time and go over your dashboard, especially when borrowing or renting a car.

Recently I rented a car at the airport and had no idea why an interior bell kept dinging. As I drove from the back of the lot to the exit, the bell would ding about four times, then stop for about ten seconds, and then start again. It was driving me crazy. I actually pulled over and sat in the rental lot for three minutes trying to figure it out. I checked my seat belt and kept looking at the dashboard for symbols until I found a symbol telling me the passenger back door was open a little bit. I never touched that door. The rental company must have left it open a crack when cleaning it.

A few things about the dashboard:

1. Check Engine Light—see a mechanic as soon as possible.
2. Low Tire Pressure Light—check your tires. Add air if needed.
3. Extra fast blinker—one of your bulbs is burnt out.
4. Red triangle—push that button when there is an emergency. It will turn on your hazard lights to warn other vehicles.

So when you get in the car, make sure you push all the necessary buttons and turn all the dials you need to before you start to drive. Make sure your doors are closed and your seat belt is on before driving. If it's hot or cold outside, then get your heater or AC going as soon as you start the car. Remember to set your mirrors and adjust your seat to the perfect position, and you'll have less to worry about when you're on the road. Also, give yourself a quick tutorial when driving an unfamiliar vehicle – especially a rental. Remember to read that owner's manual.

15
Defensive Driving

Defensive driving is the foundation of becoming a good, safe driver. Put simply, it's looking out for all the crazy drivers and being prepared to respond to their idiocy. Always remember this: defensive driving is the one gift you give to yourself that no one can take away.

If you slow down and cover your brake with your foot when you think you might get cut off in traffic, then you are driving defensively. If you scan left to right and check your mirrors, then you are driving defensively. Good job! Defensive driving is also doing all you can as a driver to diminish the chances of a crash, injury, or death.

Story Time

One guy was eating his fast food while going through a green light and got hit by a red-light runner. If that delicious cheeseburger and those crispy golden french fries hadn't taken away his concentration from the road, he could have helped himself avoid the collision. If he had been scanning left to right while approaching the intersection, he might have seen the car running the red light from his left and could have turned the steering wheel a tiny bit to the right to lessen the impact. Instead, he gave up the one gift he had for himself: his defensive driving.

Everything we teach at Spanky's Driving Academy rests upon scanning the road and being prepared to respond to other drivers. The sooner you can process a situation in your brain, the more time you have to respond to dangerous situations before they get worse. You may even have the right-of-way, but it doesn't mean the other drivers will give it to you, so pay attention and be in the moment, ready to respond to anything.

A few tips to help you drive defensively:

1. Scan left to right with your eyes. Eye movement is so important.
2. Identify what you see: bikes, pedestrians, animals, road workers, etc.
3. Predict what could happen.
4. Decide what to do about it.
5. Execute on your decision.
6. Check your rearview mirror and speedometer every five seconds so you know your speed and who's behind you.

7. Look down the road as far as possible so there aren't any surprises.

8. Slow down a little and scan left to right as you approach intersections. It could save your life!

9. Keep a safe distance behind the vehicle in front of you, and leave an opening on your left or right as an "escape" in case something happens.

10. Keep your mind and eyes on the task of driving so you are an active driver and not a passive driver.

Currently there are over forty thousand Americans dying in car crashes each year, and I'm convinced that number could be decreased by 90 percent if more drivers paid attention and drove defensively. When you drive drowsy, impaired by drugs, meds, or alcohol, or are distracted, then you are essentially throwing your gift of defensive driving out the window and saying, "I don't care enough about myself and others." But I know you do care.

Driving is all about doing the right thing while sharing the road with others. It takes a responsible person to understand what's at stake. What is at stake? People's safety and people's lives. So keep that gift close to you, and don't give it away for anything. If you remember these tips and put them into action, you'll become a really safe driver.

16
Distracted Driving

Anything that takes your mind or your eyes off the road is a distraction. Distracted driving is an epidemic in America. It's one of the biggest killers while driving a vehicle. Everywhere you look, people have their heads down buried in their phone while driving. The phone is the biggest distraction, but what else is a distraction? I can name a bunch!

1. Phone—hands-free isn't risk free
2. Food—that includes eating spaghetti
3. Music—flipping through the playlist is dangerous
4. Friends and family
5. GPS
6. Reaching for something
7. Putting on makeup

8. Shaving or grooming in some way

9. Daydreaming

According to the NHTSA, between 1966 and 1973, America had between 50,000 and 54,000 deaths in car crashes annually. That's out of a population of between 196 million and 211 million people. It took us all the way to 2014 to get that number down to about 32,000 traffic deaths a year, with a population of about 319 million. We were definitely headed in the right direction. But in 2015, those numbers started going back up. Now, as of this writing, we are up to over 40,000 car crashes per year. What's the cause of the increase? According to AAA, distracted driving is the number one cause of traffic crashes. The increase of cell phones has increased distracted driving. Talking on your hands-free device doesn't mean you won't be distracted. You can easily get focused on a conversation with someone on your Bluetooth, and that could keep you from scanning the road enough and responding to situations. Even getting caught up in your own thoughts can keep you from driving defensively. Check yourself before you wreck yourself.

Story Time

A man named Martin told me he was driving when a call came in on his hands-free device. He answered it to speak with his co-worker and ran a red light. He hit a guy in a truck, injuring him and putting him in the hospital for a few days. Martin said he saw the red light, but it didn't register in his brain because he was picturing his office and trying to remember where he placed important paperwork.

A woman in our four-hour traffic school class told me that she often gets caught up in her own thoughts and either misses a turn or an exit. She even mentioned that sometimes she doesn't remember the previous five minutes of driving because of her daydreaming. Wow!

A young person in our four-hour traffic school class told me that he looked down at his phone for what he thought was a brief second or two and didn't realize he was about to rear-end a car at the red light. Last he looked, the light was green, but he wanted to read the text really quick.

If those aren't three good stories to motivate you to stay in the moment with your thoughts, then I don't know what will.

Bad things that can happen when you are distracted:

1. You won't see things quickly enough.
2. You won't process quickly enough because you didn't see things quickly enough.
3. You won't respond quickly enough because you didn't process quickly enough.
4. You won't take the proper action because you didn't give yourself enough time to think.
5. Someone could die, and dude, that's lame!
6. Funerals might have to be planned. Lame!

People aren't just driving intoxicated; they're driving "intexticated!" Put aside anything that will distract you, and focus on getting to your job, home, school, or your BFF's house without dying—or killing someone else. Sound good? Be great!

17
DMV

What does DMV stand for? It's an acronym that stands for Department of Motor Vehicles. The DMV does quite a bit, and you'll most likely be dealing with it the rest of your driving life. Here is a short list of services the DMV provides:

1. Permit and driver's license tests
2. State identification cards
3. Vehicle titles of ownership
4. Annual registration of vehicles and updating license plates
5. Replacement of the above items that have been lost
6. Address change and new photo taken because you've moved
7. Name changes—got married?
8. Driving manuals for you to study

There may be more services provided depending on the state you live in, so check out your state's website. Some offices allow you to make an appointment, while other offices require you to grab a numbered ticket and wait in a long line until your number is called.

Some DMV offices have different names. In my state it's called the Driver Services Center, and it pretty much just helps the person get a state ID, permit, or license to drive. We go to a separate office building when we need to deal with car titles and renewing registration tags.

Call your local DMV, go online, or walk into their office to find out the exact paperwork you'll need to be able to receive the services they offer. For instance, if you need an address change because you moved, then you'll need proof of your new address, so they might require a utility bill with your name and new address on it. It helps decrease the chances of fraud. Here's a short list of documents they might require as proof for permits and licenses:

1. Primary Documents:

- Original Birth Certificate
- Original Social Security Card
- Military Identification
- Valid Passport (not expired)
- Certificate of Naturalization or Citizenship

2. Secondary Documents:

- Health Insurance Card
- Work IDs
- Printed Paycheck Stubs
- W2 Forms

You'll have to check with your local office to find out exactly what they require, so don't quote me or show them this book; all states are different. And remember, communication is key. Don't be one of those jerks who brings the wrong paperwork and decides to take his anger out on the front desk people. It's not their fault. They have a tough job, so say words like *please* and *thank you* with a smile. It might help make their day, and it might help your experience with them go smoother.

18
Driver's Education

Driver's Education (or Driver's Ed) is one of the most important classes teens can take during all their years of schooling. Think about it—driving is the most dangerous thing a teen will do on a daily basis once they get their license. I can't stress that enough.

Benefits of a quality Driver's Ed program:

1. It could lower the chances of a crash, injury, or death.
2. It could lower the chances of getting tickets.
3. It will help you become a more alert and defensive driver.

Not only can you benefit in those ways, but you will also learn about car maintenance, like when to get your tires rotated, or when to change your oil. Driver's Ed also helps teens learn about the signs and lines they'll encounter on the road. Most courses have some videos to watch, PowerPoint, classroom discussions, worksheets and quizzes. Our program offers all of those, but I include a bunch of true stories because I believe all teens need to know *why* they need to obey the law and not just what the laws are. Over the years I've noticed our teens get bored if we give them too many worksheets, but they stay engaged when you tell them a crazy story. I call it illustrative teaching.

Not all Driver's Ed classes are the same. Some programs replace two hours of real driving with a simulator, which really isn't quality driving. How can you simulate real road experience? You can't. Getting in the car with a professional driving coach will help. Knowing that you took a Driver's Ed course will boost your confidence going into your license test. You'll know that you've prepared, and you'll have that mental boost. Confidence is everything. I know of many teens who have not been prepared enough to drive and have little confidence on the road. If a teen is too tentative, the lack of decision-making can be deadly (like when making a left turn on a green light with oncoming traffic approaching). Working with a qualified driving coach can prepare you and give your confidence the boost it needs. Giving our teens repetition with lane changes and turns is key. A driving school is a partner with the parents or guardians in raising teens to be a confident defensive driver.

What to look for in a driving school:

1. Do they make defensive driving their top priority?
2. Does the program replace real driving with simulators? You paid for real driving, so you deserve real driving.
3. How much of the program is dedicated to the "non driving manual stuff," like decision-making, honoring your parents and their rules, having respect for law enforcement, and being a kind driver?
4. Do they stick you in the back seat of the car while you share time with another inexperienced teen? One-on-one driving is the best way to go.

These are just a few things to think about when choosing a program. You'll only get one shot at your Driver's Ed experience, so you don't want to have any regrets. Make some calls, ask some questions, and join a program.

19

Drowsy Driving

Do you stay up late at night? Are you on your phone so much that you're tired from a lack of sleep? Then don't get behind the wheel of a vehicle and drive. Drowsy driving is a killer. The NHTSA estimates that in 2017 there were over 90,000 police-reported crashes that involved drowsy driving, with almost 800 deaths. That is scary! Can you imagine driving along the road and suddenly seeing a car cross the yellow line into your lane, coming straight at you? That's another reason you have to drive defensively and look well down the road for approaching vehicles.

A few causes of drowsy driving:

1. Not getting enough sleep.

2. Drinking alcohol later at night. Alcohol is a depressant and can interact with sleepiness and make things worse.//
3. Taking a prescription or over-the-counter drug that can cause drowsiness.

Story Time

Years ago, a girl in Iowa named Jessie was driving late at night trying to get home from college to surprise her family for the weekend. She had already driven a couple hundred miles and had been awake for over 18 hours straight. She kept fighting off her drowsiness, but fell asleep a few exits before her turn off. Jessie went off the road. Somehow her car flipped and landed in a ditch below the road. Her car was so crushed that her foot was stuck under the dashboard. She was knocked unconscious in the crash as well. When she finally came to, she was stuck in the car for a while with no help. She finally had to break her own ankle to get her foot unstuck and crawl out the broken back window. With all her might, Jessie clawed her way in the wet soil up the embankment to the road. Two cars passed by without seeing her. Finally, a young man driving by saw her and got her to a hospital. Now that's a *crazy* story!

Here are some alternatives to drowsy driving:

1. Pull over and get some sleep. It could be at a hotel or a rest stop, but don't drive.
2. If you can, switch drivers.

3. Stop for a while, and get something to eat and drink to refresh yourself.
4. Try not to drive during the hours that you normally sleep.

Your body has its own clock. When you go without sleep for over 18 hours, it could have a similar effect on you as driving with a blood alcohol concentration of .05. That is scary, because at a .05 BAC you can start losing muscle control, have blurred vision, slurry speech, and slowed reaction time. So you can see the similarities of going without enough sleep and having alcohol in your system. Driving when you are tired IS impaired driving because you are impaired by your own drowsiness.

You are responsible for your own body. You are the one who needs to evaluate your condition to drive. It's never right to put lives at risk because you want to get to your destination sooner. The best thing to do is grab your favorite stuffed animal, cozy up in your bed, and get plenty of rest before you embark on your next adventure. Plan ahead and use wisdom.

20
Dying

Since you already know the title of this book, you should know it's no surprise that I would include chapters on dying and funerals. Sorry if I come off as a downer, but hey, this stuff needs to be addressed. Over the decades, I've learned three main things from parents of the students I teach:

1. They want to keep you safe from anything and everything that can harm you.
2. They want you to grow up and live a long, healthy life.
3. They want you to make wise choices and do something with your life that you AND they can be proud of.

That's why it is so important to talk about how fragile life can be and how it can end in the snap of a finger or blink of an eye. Millions of drivers around the world over the decades would take back "those 30 seconds" if they could to make a different decision to keep themselves and others safe and alive on the road. So many of them didn't use their driving wisdom at the time.

Story Time

Daniel was such a nice guy. He was in our driving school when he was in 10th grade. Daniel finished the classroom portion of our program with the rest of the class and even signed the wall (everyone signs one of our classroom walls and takes a photo). I still have his signature and see it every day. However, Daniel never drove the six hours with us that we recommend. He simply moved on and tested for his license without finishing the program. A couple of years later, Daniel died in a car crash. His death rocked so many in our community. Daniel died driving the same road he always drove. It's a tricky road at some points, with sweeping curves and some right side drop-offs. He's not the first teen to die on that road. I don't know how the crash happened, but it's not that important at this point. Daniel is no longer with us, and his loved ones will miss him the rest of their lives.

Another Story

Sofia was rushing to school a few days before winter break. It was finals week, and she had a couple of tests to take that morning. As she was driving down the same road she had driven for two years, Sofia crossed the yellow line, went off the left side of the road into a ditch and flipped upside down. Sofia was minutes from school and was driving just fine from her house up until the crash. What happened? The news reported that she was trying to "negotiate a curve." I know that road very well and know that there are curves on the road, so I took the report as truth. A few nights later there was a candlelight vigil at her school. It was winter, so it was dark and freezing outside, yet hundreds of people showed up and huddled together near the front of the school—most of them teens from her school. I have to honestly say that I hadn't heard wailing and crying that loud in my life. It was one of the saddest things I had ever experienced. The pain coming out of their hearts and mouths was overwhelming. Can you picture that? Try to listen to the sound of that kind of pain in your own mind. It's a tear-jerker.

Two days later I got a call at my office from a complete stranger. I guess this local dad needed to vent, so he called me, of all people. He told me he read the report that said Sofia was trying to "negotiate a curve" and he didn't believe it. He was so upset about another teen dying needlessly. He told me to drive over to the road, check the "curve," and determine for myself if it needed any "negotiating." So the next day I drove down the road and saw the skid marks and the crash site with a small memorial already set up. Sure enough, I had to agree with that dad. There were plenty of curves earlier on the road before the skid marks. Near the crash site, the road has a very slight bend in it but wouldn't be defined at all as a curve. Sofia had negotiated those earlier curves before the slight bend just fine. Did speed play a role? Was she on her phone? I don't know if anyone knows. She must have looked away from the road for a moment. I didn't read anything about her cell phone records, so I'm guessing I'll never know. But I do know that everyone misses her. That year, from Thanksgiving break to New Year's Eve we had five teens from five different schools die in our county. One teen each week was killed in a car crash. No joke! Sofia was the fourth teen to die, if I can remember correctly. I wish I had 30 seconds beforehand with each of those teens over that five-week period. It could have saved their lives. I'm sure the holidays will now hurt each year for all of their loved ones.

On behalf of your family and friends, I am literally begging you to do the RIGHT things in life. Make healthy choices—choices that make you and your family proud. No parent should have to bury their child, teen, or adult child. The offspring should always bury the parent. Dying in a car crash is one of the stupidest ways to die because most crashes are completely avoidable. Of course the studies show that more teens and young adult guys die each year than girls. Why is that? Well, as a dude, I can only say that I KNOW for a fact that I had ego, testosterone, and feelings of invincibility when I was younger. I was a good athlete and believed in my ability to do stupid stuff and come out all right. Maybe that's what puts teen guys at a higher risk.

A few tips for staying alive:

1. Spend your time doing the right things in life and not the wrong things in life.
2. Ask yourself: Could this potentially injure me or another person?
3. Don't bow down to peer pressure, and don't be the one to push the peer pressure.
4. Wear your seat belt 100 percent of the time while in a vehicle.
5. Get plenty of sleep so you are ready to drive.

6. Don't drive impaired in any way.
7. Don't drive while emotional. Emotions can get the best of you.
8. Drive defensively and expect others to do the wrong thing on the roads.

I'm sure you can add to these tips, but your entire goal each day should be to get home to your bed and pillow safely. Be the hero out there on the road and help others get home safely as well. Love and respect yourself and others enough to drive safely. Car crashes are the number one killer of teens. That's how high the stakes are. At this point you might be thinking that I am ruining this book for you, but your family and friends want you to be a safe driver and avoid having an end story like Daniel and Sofia. You are highly valuable.

21
Emergency Vehicles

What are emergency vehicles? Ambulances, police cars, motorcycles, fire trucks and other specialized vehicles that your city or county might have. If possible, when any of these vehicles have their lights and sirens on, you should pull over to the right shoulder as soon as you can and stop. Wait until they pass, and then continue. If you're on the freeway, just slow down until they pass.

If there's an emergency on the highway, most states have something called a Move Over Law. That means if there is an emergency vehicle on the shoulder, you must move a lane away from them and give at least a one-lane buffer. Check to see if anyone is in your blind spot first so you know you can switch lanes without sideswiping another vehicle or knocking a dude off his motorcycle. A blind spot is the area that you can't see in your side mirrors or with your peripheral vision. A vehicle could be there, but you can't see that it's there.

But what if you can't move over? Then slow down and pay attention to your surroundings. The emergency situation usually happens on the right shoulder. That's why it is so important to be looking down the road as far as possible and scanning left to right so there aren't any surprises.

Story Time

A few years ago, one of our students was testing for her license. Even though she learned in our class to pull over when police cars approach from the rear with lights and sirens on, she didn't do it during her driving test. Instead, she said, "Wow! I wonder where they're headed." A few moments later a second police car came from behind her, and then went around her. She said, "There must be something crazy going on up there." She didn't pull over that time, either. It was an automatic fail on her driving test. I'm sure she finally learned her lesson.

Make sure to stay out of the way of emergency vehicles. Let them do their work and move on. Don't slow down and "rubber neck" out your window, wondering what is going on, because you'll take your concentration off your own driving. In many cases, drivers not only steer with their hands but also with their eyes, and there have been MANY cases in which a driver starts to slowly turn the wheel in the direction their eyes are looking. So be careful.

Lastly, you must also yield to city buses, funeral processions, and possibly utility work vehicles. Just be aware. Be a courteous driver and let everyone get home alive.

22
Eye Movement

Scanning the road is a key point of defensive driving. Without scanning, you won't be able to identify what you see and be able to predict what could happen and make a decision on what to do. Your eyes should be moving left to right, then up at your rearview mirror every five seconds, and then down at your speedometer every five seconds, as well. Then look as far as you can down the road so you have time to respond to any situations that arise. Keep moving those eyes in that manner, and you'll be able to process what you see more quickly.

What to look for when driving:

1. Look for car doors opening from parked cars (usually on your right).
2. Try to see all the way through the back window and front windshield of the vehicle in front of you to see

what they see. You might be able to brake a little sooner, if needed, and there won't be any surprises.

3. Watch for people stepping off the curbs who might jaywalk illegally in front of you, especially in downtown areas.
4. Look over at driveways for people either backing out or leaving a parking lot.
5. Watch for vehicles coming out of alleys.
6. Check your rearview mirror every five seconds for tailgaters and emergency vehicles with lights and sirens on.

Story Time

We had an Austrian foreign exchange student named Lisa enroll in our program. Fortunately, she was scanning left to right with her eyes as she entered the four-way stop intersection. A mom on her phone, with two kids in her car, ran the stop sign and hit our car on the right side back door. Because Lisa was driving defensively by scanning left to right, she was able to turn the vehicle to the left a little bit to avoid a direct impact on the passenger front door where her driving coach was sitting. The impact was a glancing blow to the car but a $2,800 glancing blow to the mom's insurance company. Lisa was able to help the situation by paying attention and driving defensively. Her eye movement and processing helped the crash from being worse than it could have been.

23
Freeways/Interstate

Freeways, interstates and expressways are all the same thing. People in different states simply have different names for them. Freeways are multi-lane highways with limited access to enter or exit. Simply put, you really have to pay attention when merging onto the freeway. Some on-ramps are longer and some are shorter. Some on-ramps are so busy that they actually have a red and green light that switches color about every three seconds to prevent too many cars entering the freeway at the same time.

A few tips for merging:

1. Look for the gap between the vehicles you'll be merging in between.
2. Gauge the flow of traffic and match it.

3. Signal your intentions. Look in your mirror. Check your blind spot. Merge into traffic safely.
4. Pay attention so you don't run out of on-ramp.

Be very careful when merging in. Don't fight your way in and cut vehicles off. Signal early enough for other drivers to see your intentions, but also don't be passive, or you'll find yourself running out of on-ramp. You could end up driving on the shoulder, which is not good because there could be a broken-down vehicle there that you could crash into.

Once you're on the freeway, you'll probably breathe a sigh of relief because the hard part is done, but that doesn't mean you can relax and check your phone or reach for your food. While driving on the freeway can be easier than on city streets, you still need to pay attention so you don't get bored or tired because of under-stimulation to your eyes and mind. Many people like driving on the freeway better than city streets because they can set their cruise control to a specific speed and then kind of "check out," so make sure to keep paying attention.

Highway Hypnosis can occur when you become bored of the drive and there is nothing to stimulate your mind. It can happen on freeways with long stretches and little traffic. You might see the occasional road sign or driver merging on, but other than that, you could get caught up in your thoughts and then suddenly realize that you've driven ten miles and don't remember missing your exit. That's happened to many people I know. You can even start to doze off. Drivers fall asleep on the freeways at a much greater rate than on city streets because they are stopping and turning more frequently on city streets than on freeways. On winding back roads, our minds are usually focused on curves and hills, so we tend to have our heads in the game. If you are on a two-lane highway with one lane in each direction, you are going to have to really stay focused because freeways can get really dark at night without streetlights, and animals cross the road at all different times. Those back road highways can have speed limits as high as 55 miles per hour, so be careful and keep scanning the road and the roadside from left to right. It will give you a chance to respond to the animals.

Do yourself a favor and stay out of the far left lane. The far left lane is nicknamed the "fast lane" because drivers usually pass others up in that lane. Many drivers like to go faster than the legal limit, unfortunately. Speed limits vary from state to state but can go as high as 80 miles per hour in states like Montana. If you are going the speed limit in the fast lane, there is still the chance that someone will come up behind you wanting you to move over, so you might as well just stay out of the fast lane. The fast lane is also considered by police and first responders as the "number one lane" and as you move right, those lanes are the number two, number three lanes and so on. I think you get it.

The far right lane is nicknamed the "slow lane" because those drivers are either merging on and still trying to speed up to the flow of traffic, or they are slowing down to exit the freeway. The middle lane(s) are nicknamed the "through" lanes because those drivers just want to get up to speed and chill out.

Story Time

I was trying to merge on the freeway one day in Minneapolis, and traffic was going about 20 miles per hour. I was slowly running out of on-ramp and had to roll down my window and wave my hand out to get the old lady driver's attention to let me in. It appeared she was purposefully ignoring me. We ended up about five feet from each other, and I yelled from my open window to her open window, "Hi there, beautiful! May I get over please?" She looked over at me, smiled, and waved me in. It was that easy.

Having eye contact with other drivers and being kind is a big part of the driving life. It might be hard for you to do, but what do you want? Do you want bad experiences on the road or good experiences? Sometimes it feels easier to be mean, but it takes a lot of energy out of you when you really think about it. We need more heroes out there. I hope you are one of them. Be safe and enjoy the drive!

24
Fun

Let's talk about the fun part of having a driver's license. I smell freedom! I smell independence! How cool is that? Having that license will open up a whole new world for you. It can provide a lot of ways for you to have fun. You might be able to get a job and get some money in your pocket. That's fun! You might be able to spend more time with your friends going to a movie, the mall, or the pool. That's fun, too! You won't have to rely on a train, subway, bus, or bike to get you around. You can come and go when you want and won't have to depend on anyone else. You will have more freedom with a driver's license than you had before.

Story Time

Getting a license and a car provided my buddy Glenn with a lot more freedom. His parents worked a lot, so Glenn had a lot of time on his hands to play sports and do fun things with that little, yellow, awesome car. We used to go to the donut shop together or to the pizza place to hang out with friends. We were even allowed to drive one hour away to the water park for the day or to go skiing with our buddy Sick Rob.

As a young adult, I had a really nice sports car. A five-speed stick shift Mitsubishi Eclipse. It had a hatchback, so I could load my mountain bike and hit the trails or the bike path at Venice Beach. I would hit the mountain bike trails with my buddies Danny and Tom up in the mountains near Malibu beach and even drive down to San Diego, as well. If it was cold outside, I would drive with the windows rolled down and the heater turned on high. I just liked driving a lot. Today, not so much. I drive a lot for work with teens, and when I'm not in the car, I'm pretty much with my family. However, I've been restoring a 1999 Chevy Tahoe for many years now. My Tahoe has just the basics in it, without an auxiliary port for music. Just a CD player, an old-school cassette player, and the radio. That SUV brings me a lot of joy and fun, and it has been a labor of love getting it painted, having a new air conditioner installed, buying new snow tires, and many other things. My daughters drive it to school often, and it's been a hit with their friends. With the world slowly moving toward electric vehicles, this old Tahoe will become a classic in the next few years.

A few tips for having fun with a car:

1. When having fun driving around, make sure you don't overload your car with passengers.

2. Don't get distracted; maintain concentration on driving.

3. Keep wearing that seat belt.

4. Don't drive with your left foot up on the dashboard or on your seat. Have both feet on the floorboard near your pedals.

5. Enjoy this great time in your life. Takes some pictures of yourself with your car because it may not be the same car you own years down the road.

6. The better you take care of your vehicle, the more enjoyable it will be. Maintain it well.

Driving is fun. Enjoy it, but be mature and responsible, or you can end up being a statistic that others read about. Just be cool.

25
Funerals

So, this is not a topic I like to talk about…ever. It's tough, and it's sad, and no one should have to bury their loved one because of a stupid car crash. One California Highway Patrol officer said we shouldn't call car crashes "accidents" because an accident is something that is really out of our control, something that we didn't have a say in. A car crash is something that can be avoided most of the time. So I've been referring to car accidents as car collisions or car crashes for the past fifteen years. Perhaps we should actually call them car negligence. I don't think that would work because most people want to diminish their responsibility when they do something wrong; that's why most people say, "It was an accident. I didn't mean to do that."

    The problem is when people are not driving in a safe and responsible way, bad things can happen, like crashes, injuries, or even death. Have you ever been to a funeral for a person who was killed in a car crash? I'm telling you, they are a lot different than a funeral for an 85-year-old whose heart gave out because of old age.

I've been a chaplain for a long time and was on staff for a couple of years at a nursing home, so I've experienced older people being on hospice when nearing their last days. I've officiated weddings, baptisms, and funerals for many people over the years, and each has its own experience and emotions attached to it. But a funeral for a young car crash victim is a different level of emotion.

Believe me, your family and other loved ones care about you so much and are counting on you to do the right thing when driving any kind of motor vehicle. I know of parents who are paralyzed by fear of what could happen to their teen, so they delay them getting their license. They simply are not ready for that kind of danger.

The most dangerous thing a teen will do on a daily basis is drive to school and work, so I'm going to spend more time on this chapter making sure my words have a better chance of sinking into your brain and your heart to motivate you to be a safe driver.

Story Time

Luke was a good soccer player and had just finished a Driver's Ed program in his town. He had goals and dreams and a bright future. Each week he would attend our Sunday school Bible study class with his buddy and plop down on one of the bean bag chairs for the hour or so. He was such a nice guy. Very kind. I didn't know him very well but was so happy to see him each week. Evidently, he liked coming to the class and learning about what God wanted to do in his life.

One night I got a call from our senior pastor saying that Luke was killed in a car crash. I was floored. I had just turned 40—had a nice birthday present with the best gift of all, the birth of our miracle baby girl Alexa eight days before. I was riding high on life as the daddy of a third daughter. All the while, across the river another family was grieving the loss of their son.

It turns out Luke's dad was driving their pickup truck very aggressively and didn't insist on Luke wearing a seat belt since he didn't have one on either. The dad tried passing up two cars illegally and clipped one of them, which caused him to go off the road, flipping the truck. Both father and son were ejected. Luke's dad crawled around in the dark field looking for Luke, and when he found him, he held him as he died in his arms.

I feel horrible actually telling this story fifteen years later because I've never put it on paper before. It's doing weird things to me now looking back on those days and weeks. Luke's mom asked me to deliver the eulogy at Luke's celebration of life service (funeral). I was so nervous that night walking through the parking lot, with the temperature at about fifteen degrees in November. That night the church was packed so full that all his high school soccer teammates stood alongside the walls of the church. They all decided to wear their soccer uniforms to honor Luke. They had a couple hundred extra chairs outside of the sanctuary lined up down the hall, with a special screen hooked up for the rest of the people to see.

I talked about Luke's short life of love, friendship and sports. Luke's mom and dad were both in the front row with his 12-year-old sister sitting between them. Luke's parents were divorced because of the dad's drug and alcohol issues.

I can't help but wonder what Luke's mom was thinking about her ex-husband while she was burying her son. Luke's dad had a bunch of scabs on the side of his face and ear, and he sat there looking numb and stunned. Perhaps he was still in shock at what he had done. All 1,500 of those people were there because of one man's horrible decision, a decision based out of impatience and ego. Because of that decision, a ton of lives were forever changed.

Today my daughter Alexa is sixteen years old and is starting to drive. It's an awesome time for both of us, and I don't take these days for granted. Luke's mom didn't have that opportunity. The family was blessed with a bench dedicated in Luke's honor placed near the soccer field. Luke was hoping to have his family attend his graduation ceremony three years later, but instead they attended his funeral. A funeral that did not have to happen. Let that sink in.

Here are a few life tips for you:

1. Live a long, healthy life making wise decisions.
2. Leave your ego at home when you drive.
3. Don't be an idiot driver, and don't be a passenger with an idiot driver.
4. Understand what's at stake—your life!—and how important it is for you to be a safe and responsible driver.
5. Wear your seat belt.
6. Don't break your family's heart. They may never recover.

I don't mean to drag you down with a second chapter around the topic of death. I just want to make it crystal clear that you have a lot to lose when you drive in an unsafe manner. Take your time, drive defensively, and remember that we are all just trying to get from point A to point B safely. In the end, everyone will die and have a funeral of some sort. Make great choices, be kind to people both inside the car and out, and leave a long legacy of love behind. Aim for dying when you are old and grey. That way people will celebrate you and be thankful for you because you left a wonderful impact on others.

26
Getting into the Car

You might be thinking that you shouldn't need a chapter on getting into the car, but actually there's a lot of things to think about before you get out on the road.

A few tips when getting behind the wheel:

1. Put all unnecessary things away, like wallet, purse, phone or backpack.

2. Put the key in the ignition and start the car—unless you have a push button ignition.

3. If you start the car first, you can get your air conditioner or heater going so that you can actually think and not start to get really cold or start to sweat.

4. Adjust your seat by moving the bottom part forward and backward and then the back part up or back.

5. Adjust your rearview mirror and side mirrors. Put your hands on the steering wheel at the 9 and 3 position and move your eyes to see in all three mirrors. You should only need to shift your eyes up to look in the rearview mirror but move your head left or right to look in your side mirrors.

6. Now that you're comfortable, the seat fits well, and the mirrors work well, you can put on your seat belt. Make sure it's over your shoulders and across your chest. The lap portion should fit across your hips. Don't let it ride up on your stomach.

7. Check your instrument panel to see if any lights are on that shouldn't be, like low oil or the check engine light. If so, then drive to a mechanic and have them check it out for you.

Personally, I don't like to be restrained with the seat belt when I'm trying to move around adjusting things and putting things in place. In all the decades I've driven cars, I've never had one take off on me while the gearshift is in park. If you have a manual stick shift car, then you might put your seat belt on first since you have to have your stick shift in neutral and use the clutch to start the car. But only 1 percent of the cars now sold in the United States are stick shift, so we are massively phasing them out. Some people might be sad about that.

I've had a few teens this past year put the car keys on their leg, and then the keys fall down into the abyss between the seat and center console. It's a pain in the butt trying to reach down there to get them. Meanwhile, the car is getting hotter by the second because the AC isn't on yet. So I think you can understand my reasoning for starting the vehicle up as soon as you get in and close the door.

Once you've done all that, you are ready to roll. The big thing is to take a second and think about what you are going to do next. Are you backing down the driveway? Are you pulling away from the curb? Are you headed to school, work or a friend's house? Think about where you are about to drive, determine which route you have to take, and you will be ready to roll.

27
Impaired Driving

This subject is one of the most important topics in this entire book. Remember: driving is the most dangerous thing a new driver is going to do on a daily basis. When you add anything to your system that can alter your body or your mind, it can greatly affect your driving ability. Many people think impaired driving means we are only talking about alcohol. But the letters DWI (Driving While Impaired), DUI (Driving Under the Influence), and OWI (Operating While Intoxicated or Operating While Impaired) are used by different states to describe driving while under the influence of anything that impairs—or diminishes—your ability to drive.

Some things that can cause impairment:

1. Alcohol
2. Marijuana

3. Cocaine

4. Painkillers

5. Sleeping aids

6. Over the counter medications

7. Cold medicines

8. Drowsiness

There are many other things that can impair your ability to drive. You can do your own research on the subject, but I'm sure you get the point. Driving a motor vehicle is a great responsibility, and putting anything in your system that takes away from you being the best driver you can be is flat-out irresponsible. You are unnecessarily putting lives at risk, and law enforcement has a huge issue with that. So do I.

While reading this, I want you to think about how many people are driving at this very moment with some sort of drug or alcohol in their system. Would you like to be hit and possibly injured by one of those impaired drivers? I don't think so. You would demand justice, and rightly so.

The legal age to drink alcohol in most states is twenty-one. If you are underage, you should honor the law, honor your parents, and honor yourself by doing the right thing and waiting to drink until you are legally allowed. I've had many friends over the years become addicted to alcohol and/or drugs, and it ruined their lives and hurt their relationships with others. In every case, they were teenagers when they started. Looking back to high school, I remember specific classmates who would party like rock stars. It went from a casual beer while trying to fit in to multiple shots of vodka to major binge drinking.

It went from cigarettes to marijuana to LSD and cocaine. What started out as just partying with their friends quickly spiraled out of control into addiction. And some of those friends drove while they were drunk or high on drugs.

Once you have a couple of drinks or take a drug, your judgment begins to decrease and you get a false sense of courage. Your reaction time and clearness of vision are also impaired. That's where the car comes into play. You might think you can drive home safely, but that's the alcohol or drug lying to you. Car crashes are the leading cause of death among teens. According to the NHTSA, a whopping twenty-seven percent of drivers between the ages of fifteen and twenty years old who were killed in car crashes in 2021 had alcohol in their system.

Story Time

An underaged guy named Michael and his two buddies made some really bad fake IDs and used them to buy a 12-pack of beer. Well, Michael drank six of the beers himself and was so hammered that he crashed the car and killed his two friends. They planned the evening, lied to their parents about their plans, and even drove to a different county to use the fake IDs. The entire evening was a bad plan from the start. Michael ended up getting a ten-year jail sentence that was suspended after he served four years. That means he was on probation without a license to drive for the remaining six years. He also had to do 1000 hours of community service. If he got caught doing just one thing that was against the law, he would have to go back and serve the remaining six years. To this day, he lives with the guilt of his horrible decision-making. If he had just one minute back, I'm sure he would have chosen not to drive that evening.

A few tips about drinking:

1. Don't drink at all—you are underage.
2. Don't get in the car with someone who is impaired by anything.
3. Get a ride home from someone who is sober.
4. Always keep your parents in the loop of what you are doing.
5. If you do drink, then don't drive. Call your parents.
6. If you are sober, then be the one to drive if you have a license.
7. Make healthy choices for yourself. Use wisdom.

    I have more stories of people being ruined by drugs or alcohol, but they would take up too many pages in this book. By the way, alcohol IS a drug. Not sure if you knew that. It just happens to be in liquid form. It is way too risky to have any alcohol in your system or in your vehicle when driving. The last thing you want to do is bring your impairment into a car and drive. You could do horrible damage to yourself or others. You could do prison time, hospital time or be dead in the morgue waiting to be identified by your family. Just stay away from it. My advice is the same for other types of recreational drug use. Just stay away from them. You have too many gifts and talents to waste by being impaired by drugs, and you have better things to do with your time.

    Marijuana is now legal in many states, and it only adds more problems for law enforcement. Getting high can severely impair your driving, just like alcohol, so stay away from it. It can impair your ability to judge distance, and it also decreases your coordination. Weed also takes away your motivation, which is a disservice to you and your ability to go after your future dreams. Plus, you'll just look like some loser stoner. Who wants that reputation on them? I've been around stoned people and am embarrassed for them because they don't know whether they're coming or going. You are better than that.

Drugs and alcohol take you away from succeeding in life. When you add a motor vehicle to the situation, all sorts of bad things can happen. Your family loves you very much and wants the best for you. They want you to make healthy choices in life that will leave a legacy of good things. They want you to thrive. Don't let drugs or alcohol keep you from doing so.

28

Insurance

Car insurance is a must-have in this country. Most states require car insurance as proof of financial responsibility if you crash into another vehicle. Perhaps your parents will strike a deal with you that you pay for the car insurance if they buy you the car. Perhaps you'll have to pay for all of it, including gas. The minimum amount of insurance most states require is called liability insurance. Liability covers the other driver's car if you crash into it. However, liability doesn't pay for your car. You'll need additional insurance to cover your car. My teen daughters have full coverage on the Chevy Tahoe. They are even covered in case they drive another person's car. So that brings us to the question of what's really insured—the vehicle or the driver? Well, the answer is: kinda both. The price of insurance varies with each car. If you have a very expensive newer Tesla with 1,300 miles, then it will cost you more to have insurance coverage on it than a ten-year-old Buick with 90,000 miles on it. It also depends a little bit on where you live. Do you think that downtown New York City has higher rates than sleepy College Grove, TN, population 5,500? Of course. So you'll have to shop around for good coverage at a reasonable price. If you are a safe driver with no tickets, your rates will be lower than the rate of someone who's been in a crash and has two tickets on her record.

A few tips for finding an insurance company:

1. Get quotes from different insurance companies.
2. Determine what kind of coverage they offer and what you need.
3. Check online ratings, if that's important to you.
4. Ask if they give discounts for good grades or Driver's Ed.

Another thing that affects your insurance payment is the deductible. A deductible is the amount you pay out of your own pocket before the insurance company pays the rest. Example: You have a $1,000 deductible and you get into a crash that costs $1,500 to fix. You pay $1,000, and the insurance company will pay the remaining $500. If your deductible amount is $500, the insurance company would pay $1,000 of that $1,500 charge. But the lower the deductible, the higher you will pay in monthly premiums (your monthly insurance payment). Yes, it sounds expensive. But if you don't get into a crash that's your fault, then you won't have to pay out anything extra other than your monthly premium payment.

I have a $1,000 deductible on each of our cars, with full coverage as well. Full coverage means the insurance company will pay for things like theft, hail damage, vandalism, and also repairs to your car (collision coverage). Your car insurance will also pay for medical payments if you injure yourself or someone else. Believe me, you'll want that "safety net" in case anything ever happens. I won't go into what each coverage means. You can check them out online when looking for an insurance carrier. I tell my daughters and our students to always have full coverage on their future vehicles because they can sleep at night knowing they are covered—even if a bozo without insurance runs into them. Yes, it may be a little bit more expensive per month, but you'd rather have that peace of mind knowing you are fully covered. In the end, car insurance is the one product you own that you hope you never have to use. If you spend your time doing all the right and safe things on the road, you won't have time to do the wrong things out there. Use wisdom, dudes. Obey the law, and be safe, girls!

29
Intersections

According to the National Highway Administration, each year about one-quarter of traffic deaths and about one-half of all traffic injuries in the United States happen at intersections. That's why it is so important for you to really pay attention when approaching them.

Story Time

One day I was in my car waiting at a red light when I was rear-ended by a guy. We were both uninjured, so we drove both cars over to the gas station parking lot. My back bumper was smashed in, and there was some damage to his front end. I called the police for them to come out and fill out an incident report. The cop arrived and gave the other driver a ticket for hitting me. His insurance paid to fix my car over the next few weeks, and we all moved on with our lives. It turns out the guy wasn't paying attention while approaching the intersection and didn't realize we were all stopped at a red light. I don't know what took his eyes and mind off the road. I do remember passing by him as he was waiting to turn out of a fast-food joint because I watched to make sure he didn't turn out in front of me. He let me go by and then turned right out of the parking lot and rear-ended me. Perhaps he looked down to grab one of his crispy, golden brown french fries. Ha!

A few tips on dealing with intersections:

1. Scan with your eyes left to right as you approach the intersection. It will help you identify a potential red-light runner.

2. Take your foot off your gas pedal as you approach an intersection and cover your brake with your foot just in case someone runs a red light from your left or right.

3. Glance briefly in your rearview mirror to see how close vehicles are behind you in case you have to brake hard for a red-light runner or a vehicle turning in front of you.

4. When you see a yellow light, make every reasonable effort to stop.

5. Some residential intersections have no stop signs because of low traffic. They are called uncontrolled intersections, so you have to slow down, stop if necessary, and give the right-of-way. Be careful not to fly through them.

With so much happening at intersections, it's important that you pay close attention when approaching them. Don't change lanes or try to pass up vehicles when going through them. Don't try to beat the yellow light; only continue through if you can't stop in a reasonable manner. At four-way stop intersections, whoever arrives first has the right-of-way. You must allow them to go first. If you both arrive at the same time, then the vehicle on the right has the right-of-way. If four cars arrive at the same time, then usually there will be a more assertive driver who will inch forward a little bit, and then everyone usually lets them go first. Then it's the right-hand rule for the other three vehicles. Feel free to use your hand to wave people on and smile, letting them know they can go because sometimes drivers just sit there not knowing the law.

More intersections are being made as roundabouts. Those are circle intersections where you give the right-of-way (yield) to vehicles in the roundabout before entering. Roundabouts help traffic move more smoothly and keep traffic from backing up too far while everyone takes their turn having to stop completely at a stop sign. Over the years, I've found that most parents of my students don't drive through roundabouts with their teens, so many teens don't know what to do when they arrive at one. If you have any roundabouts in your area, then get some practice driving through them.

30

Kindness

Kindness goes a long way, especially in driving. On any given day, there are more drivers cutting each other off and tailgating than waving and letting someone merge in front of them. Being kind on the roads can help you stay calm and keep your sanity. You never know what someone's history is five minutes before encountering them on the road. For all you know, a person may have just found out their brother died. Yes, they are supposed to be paying attention on the road, but they are probably thinking more about their loved one at that moment than driving, and they might cut you off without signaling. No need to flip that driver off. Just forgive them, show kindness, and move on. Cutting a person off isn't always on purpose, but revenge always is.

Story Time

Back in the late '90s I was stopped behind a guy at a red light when his car suddenly stalled and started to back up traffic.

Many of us were stopped too close to each other and couldn't maneuver around him. A few of us got out of our cars and teamed up to push his car around the corner and out of traffic. Within a minute or so we were all on our way and the guy called AAA to come help him. It was such a small act of kindness on our part, but he'll never forget the kindness we showed him that day.

A few tips to help you show kindness:

1. Wave and say thank you to others who let you in when you want to merge.
2. Be the hero and let others in when they are trying to merge in front of you.
3. Be patient when others appear lost or are going too slow for your liking.
4. Be forgiving when others apologize to you and send a quick smile.
5. Offer help to others if you have the ability to.

We need more heroes on the roads. Generally, drivers are selfish and only think about getting to their destination without thinking of others, but we are all in this together. Driving with a "team" mindset will help everyone get where they need to go in a safe manner. So dude, don't be an idiot. Be kind!

31
Lane Changes

Lane changes can be very tough for the new driver. There's a lot going on in your brain at any given moment, so to ask you to change lanes can throw a wrench into your thought process. For some reason, many teens I work with automatically press the brake pedal about the same time they put on their blinker. I'm still trying to figure that one out. I think it's just a brain thing. Some teens think the blinker should go on right before they change lanes, but you should actually put the blinker on sooner to let the other drivers know that you WANT to change lanes—not that you are ACTUALLY changing lanes at that moment. Some of our teens will put the blinker on and immediately try to move over without even checking their blind spot for clearance. Most of the time, I'm on top of it and can remind them quickly enough not to move until they know it's clear. I'm always checking the blind spot anyway to help them out. Remember, a blind spot is the area around your vehicle that you can't see with your side mirrors or your peripheral vision.

Story Time

I was a very lazy driver back in my 20s. On a few different occasions, I almost hit cars by not checking my blind spot. One time I was moving one lane over to my left. I put my left signal on but looked over my left shoulder to check my blind spot AS I was changing lanes instead of before changing lanes. I almost sideswiped a really nice, red mustang and put a bunch of dents in it. Thank goodness the other driver honked his horn and caught my attention. He was driving defensively and saved me from messing up both of our cars. It was just plain laziness that almost caused a crash.

A few tips to help you with lane changes:

1. Turn on your blinker early enough to allow the drivers in the next lane to see it. Most people drive passively and may not see your blinker until it's been on for a few ticks, so give them a little bit of time or you might startle them.
2. Make sure there is enough of a gap for you to change lanes without being too close to the car in front of you or cutting the car off behind you. Be safe.
3. Look in your side mirror to help you see the lane you want to enter.
4. Look over the correct shoulder to eliminate the blind spot.
5. Safely change lanes and turn your blinker off.

Lane changes are a part of driving that takes a lot of repetition to do well. Practice makes progress, and you might surprise yourself how quickly you master it. One way to fail your license test is to not look over your shoulder before changing lanes. In many states it's called a "critical error." Imagine knocking a guy off his motorcycle because you didn't see him in your blind spot. That will be a bad day for everyone, especially the biker. So take your time. Don't rush your lane changes. Be safe out there.

32

Lane Control

Lane control is an essential skill to master to pass your driving test. The goal in driving is to stay centered in the lane while maintaining a safe speed. I drive with many teens who have very novice lane control skills and require me using my left hand to stabilize the steering wheel so we don't go into the ditch or clip a car going the opposite direction. Can you imagine how scary that is? Perhaps you do that to your parents. You might be giving them a heart attack. Poor Mom!

Recently, I was driving with a teen girl who kept getting too close to the curb. Most of the time the speed limit was 35 miles per hour, so imagine hitting the curb at that speed! We could have popped a tire or messed up the axle. Another teen I was coaching would drive consistently too close to the left yellow line and oncoming traffic. Those are the times when parents start freaking out on their teens. They grab that "scream handle" or hit the invisible "fake brake."

Story Time

Katie only had her license for about one year. She was on her way home from hanging out with her boyfriend and his parents. As Katie was driving in the dark and perhaps a little passively, her tires went off the road a little bit and she panicked and jerked the wheel back to the left. The car went across oncoming traffic and hit a huge boulder, and Katie died. Had Katie been paying attention and kept her lane control, she probably would be alive today.

A few tips for staying centered:

1. Practice, practice, practice—practice makes progress, and soon you'll develop muscle memory, and your lane control will be more consistent.
2. Left is death, right is life.
3. Pay attention. If you are paying attention and stay on your game, you will see how often you drift to the right or left and can make the adjustment. Don't allow your eyes or mind to wander. Always be self-aware.

If anything, be thankful if you tend to drift a little to the right rather than left. Drivers are distracted, tired, etc. and occasionally drive too close to the yellow line. So stay away from it when cars go by. Just be careful you don't clip the curb on the right. If your right tires go off the road a little bit onto the gravel, then slowly take your foot off the gas pedal and bring your tires back onto the road. Don't freak out and jerk the steering wheel to the left, or your car will go into oncoming traffic. There also could be a four-foot ditch on the right, and your car could possibly end up crashing in it. So watch out! I always tell our teens that I would rather go in a ditch than hit another oncoming car, especially if there are kids in it or it's a giant cement truck. But you don't want issues on either side. Keep practicing, and you'll see improvement in your lane control in no time.

33
License Test—The BIG day!

This is what you've been waiting for! You may have talked about it repeatedly with your besties, and you have put in the time and the miles to get to the big day. All that time and energy. All that anxiety and fear. All the confidence and excitement will now reveal itself! You are now about to get to the start line to begin your driving career! As easy as the driving test can be, you can still have a brain fart and do the wrong thing. In my experience, the more miles a teen practices, the more their ability and confidence goes up. You have to remember that it's just a five- to ten-minute driving test in most states. Don't freak yourself out! You've got this! You've driven longer stretches with your parents. You've been on the interstate and through a ton of intersections. You have the ability.

Each state has its own driving test route and things they'll test you on, but these are the basics:

1. Backing out of the parking lot
2. Left and right turns
3. Lane changes
4. Possible parallel parking

Story Time

Landon was just about to turn 18 and his dad made an appointment to have him test for his license. Landon told his parents repeatedly that he wasn't ready to test. It was obvious he wasn't ready; his parents rarely practiced with him because they were consumed with their jobs and didn't make the time to invest in Landon. Poor Landon started out his test by backing out and slamming into a parked car. Test over. It was an automatic fail. The parents only had themselves to blame.

A few tips for test day:

1. Wear deodorant. You might sweat with nerves before you even arrive to test.
2. Wear comfortable clothes and have your hair out of your eyes so you can see clearly. Don't wear flip flops. Wear a basic sneaker.
3. Remember and dwell on all the miles and hours you have put in up to this point.
4. Use a vehicle that you are very comfortable driving and have practiced with.
5. Make sure the registration tags are current and all the lights and gauges are working properly.

6. Know where everything is located because they usually ask—starting with the lights and hazard lights. This is VERY important, so go over the entire dashboard, gearshift, seat belt, and mirrors very thoroughly with your parent or guardian. Make sure the horn works as well.

7. Bring your permit to show the test examiner. Don't forget!

Some teens don't have enough training under their belt and then freak out when it comes time to test. You can't fake being a good driver. Practice makes progress, but it doesn't make perfect. It takes time just to become an average driver, and if parents don't take the time to invest in the most dangerous thing a teen will do on a daily basis, disaster might happen. In Landon's case, the parents had to pay for the other car, and it was a ding on their insurance.

If you dwell on all the successes you had during the time you had your permit, it will help your brain and keep your confidence up. Even though some of our teens have the ability to pass the test and drive independently, they still make crucial mistakes—like pulling out in front of another car—and fail their test. Don't be your own worst enemy. You've grown so much as a driver and can pass that driving test! Just work the process and believe in your ability. Good luck!

34
Maintaining Your Vehicle

Taking care of your vehicle is not just good common sense, it's a matter of life and death. Imagine driving your car on two extremely worn front tires and hydroplaning in the rain and crashing. You might hurt yourself or another person, or you might do something worse, like kill someone. Now imagine sitting in the court room begging the judge and jury to forgive you because you simply made a "mistake" by waiting too long to buy new tires. You didn't mean to be lazy, but you were so "busy" that you couldn't find the time.

Being lazy can cost lives. Many crashes occur because of an owner's laziness to get new brakes or new tires or new anything because they don't want to spend the money or be without the vehicle for a day or two. It's better to budget and have a savings account for fixing things rather than put those things off.

Story Time

When two of our daughters were new teen drivers, they took turns driving the 1999 Chevy Tahoe I mentioned earlier that I was slowly restoring. The truck was old, with 225,000 miles on it, and needed some work. We put on four brand-new snow tires, put in a new AC and heater, gave it a brand-new paint job, and a few other things. I loved that SUV! I looked at the oil change reminder sticker in the top left of the windshield and noticed it was about time for the 3,000-mile oil change and for the fluids to be refilled. It was summer, and the girls used the air conditioner a lot. That meant the coolant was running low and more needed to be poured into the radiator. Sure enough—both daughters thought the other would get it all taken care of. One day, the engine overheated, with a ton of steam coming out. The radiator and engine were both history. We found a used engine with 119,000 miles on it and bought a new radiator along with it, all for $2,000. That was actually a good deal, because it also included removal of the old engine! But it was still an extra and unnecessary cost. The girls learned a lesson; they now keep an eye on the mileage sticker and get the oil changed every 3,000 miles with the fluids refilled.

A few tips for maintaining your vehicle:

1. Rotate your tires every 7,500 miles, and walk around your vehicle every few days to check for any nails, screws, or glass embedded in your tires.
2. Have your oil changed each time according to your vehicle manufacturer. Usually, it's every 3,000 miles for regular oil and 5,000 miles for synthetic oil,

although synthetic is a little more expensive. Have them check all your other fluids at that same time.

3. Change your wiper blades every six to twelve months, depending on where you live and according to how often you'll use them. Since rubber is degradable, the blades won't be as effective as time goes by.

4. Read the owner's manual on your vehicle to see when certain maintenance checkups should be done. Some things need to be checked every 30,000, 50,000 or 60,000 miles.

5. Keep your car washed regularly to keep stuff from hurting the paint job or under the car, like salt from the salt trucks in states that have a lot of snow.

6. Clean your headlights once a month. Over time, headlights can become oxidized and a film can form over the outside of the headlights which makes them emit less light. I've replaced entire headlights a couple of times over the years, and they can cost about $120 per pair, or more.

7. Occasionally have a reputable local mechanic check your vehicle out and provide a list of things that might need to be taken care of. If we go to the doctor occasionally for a check-up, then why not do it for our vehicles, since we rely on them so much from day to day?

So the moral of the story is to take good care of your vehicle because you rely on it so much. Treat it like a family member and keep it as long as you can. Take pride in your vehicle and enjoy driving it. Perhaps give it a name. Our Tahoe is named Carl. I'm going to keep Carl around for a long time.

35
Motorcycles

I've mentioned before that most drivers are passive drivers, meaning they usually don't have their full attention on everything that driving requires. Driving is multitasking in and of itself, so you really have to be on the ball when out there on the road. If you don't have your mind on driving, then we all suffer at some point. One very vulnerable person who suffers is the motorcycle rider. Research shows that two-thirds of motorcycle-car collisions are caused by the driver of a car who turns in front of a motorcycle. That's scary, dude! The motorcyclist is at a huge risk when out there on the road, especially at intersections.

Motorcycles are hard to see. They are narrow and sometimes blend in with the scenery. They test a driver's depth perception, and it's hard to know how close they are to us. In all my driving years, I've noticed that about 90 percent of the motorcycle riders I've encountered were speeding, so I've had to watch out for them. One moment they're 500 feet behind me on the freeway, and the next moment they are flying past me. However, there are also the casual bikers who just want to get from A to B safely. I've noticed they are usually the older riders who've survived over the decades and just want to make it to 90 years old where they can die of old age in their own bed. I'll take that over a crash any day!

Story Time

When I was about 11 years old, my parents allowed me to have a minibike. I believe it was a little, red Yamaha 50 with no muffler. I also had a 1960s orange helmet with no chin guard or plastic face protector—only a chin strap. That little minibike was loud! I probably woke the entire block up while riding it on early summer mornings. Looking back on it, I'm surprised I wasn't hit by a car backing out of their driveway while I flew that bike up and down my street. One day, my friend's mom from across the street came out of her house to tell me she was very concerned for my safety and to be extra careful because I was so small and difficult for everyone to see. Her 15-year-old son had died a few years earlier while riding his motorcycle in the hills around the corner from our neighborhood, and to this day I don't think she ever got over it. The minibike had engine issues to begin with and finally sputtered out on me, so I moved on to riding my skateboard and playing Atari the rest of the summer. That was probably a good thing.

In my senior year (1985) I wore that same orange helmet while riding my yellow twenty-dollar moped around town until it finally gave out on me. Then it was back to the ten-speed bike. However, my buddy Tom had a really cool, red Kawasaki

GPZ 550. One day we ditched fifth and sixth period to hit the beach. **NOTE: Don't ditch school, dudes and dudettes! Your families are expecting you to be where you are supposed to be—in class! Ok, back to the story.** As Tom headed to the student parking lot, I climbed the fence back by the auto shop class and hopped on the back of his bike. We flew through Malibu Canyon to the beach to play some volleyball and body surf near the pier. I decided to take my shirt off and just wore my shorts and shoes for the ride. We were young, free living, and didn't care THAT day for helmets. How stupid!

After an hour or so at the beach, we came back to the Valley and stopped by Tom's house, grabbed a sandwich and headed down the hill back to the school to watch the girls play softball. On the way down the hill at about 35 miles per hour, the clutch cable snapped and the back tire of the motorcycle started shaking back and forth. I had not put my shirt back on, so I kept thinking the bike would tip and I would get road rash like cheese on a cheese grater. Picture that! After a few seconds, Tom got the bike into neutral, the shaking stopped, and we coasted the rest of the way down the hill to the traffic light at Valley Circle Boulevard. Tom pushed the bike onto the sidewalk, put the kickstand down, and we both looked at each other with a collective sigh. We lived! Yep! That was us in 1985 for you. There was no helmet law in California back then. But just because something is not a law doesn't mean we shouldn't do the safe thing—correct? That's a great question to ask yourself. Driving or riding a motorcycle is all about getting from A to B in the safest manner possible while lowering the chances of a crash, injury or death. That's driving in general. That's the pact you have to make with yourself.

Less than a year later, Tom and I were living in Oceanside. He had moved on from the GPZ to a Chevy pick-up truck. I was on the prowl for a motorcycle of my own, so we went to the dealership to check them out. I saw a really sharp Kawasaki KZ 550 that had some stellar orange pinstripes on the gas tank, so I went into the accessories shop to look at upgrading my old orange 60s helmet for perhaps a 1980s new orange one. Up on the shelf were a bunch of helmets ranging from $50 to $250. When I asked the sales dude what the difference between a fifty-dollar helmet and a two-hundred-and-fifty-dollar helmet was, he simply asked me, "Well dude, how much is your head worth?" HA! How much was my head *really* worth? So I told him I would go home and think about it. After a few days, I determined my head was worth *more* than $250, so I didn't buy the motorcycle, and it was a very wise choice. Unlike the one I made involving the train. Uh—you can read about that when you get to the Trains chapter. At any rate, I'm really glad I didn't buy that motorcycle.

Another Story

My mentor, Pastor Bob, has a son my age named Paul. When we were in our early 40s, Paul was riding his motorcycle with his helmet on when a small pick-up truck turned left in front of him. Paul hit the truck and flew over the handlebars, colliding with the truck. Paul almost died and ended up with a traumatic brain injury. Speaking on the phone with his mom Marion a couple of weeks later, she told me that the other driver never apologized for turning in front of Paul. I heard the pain in her voice over the phone, and it broke my heart. Paul hasn't worked since, and it took about five years before he could actually stand at the sink and wash a bowl by hand with a sponge. They are such a great family, and it's tough that they had to deal with such a tragedy.

A few tips for dealing with motorcyclists:

1. Stay back more than the required three-second following distance. Especially in poor weather. You don't want to run over the motorcyclist if they lay their bike down on a wet road.
2. Don't allow them to get into your blind spots.
3. Double-check and really look for motorcycles when turning left.
4. When in traffic, watch for bikes splitting the lanes and coming very close to your side mirrors. Many bikes ride in between the cars, only a few inches from cars. Lane splitting is allowed by law in fewer than ten states. It's dangerous and puts everyone at risk.

So to wrap this chapter up, PLEASE watch out for motorcycles. And if you ever buy a motorcycle, then be the best defensive rider you can be, because the odds are usually stacked against you. Your family and friends love you and want you to stick around for a long time. So dude, don't die!

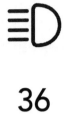

36
Night Driving

Night driving can be very dangerous if you don't keep your head in the game. Many drivers don't change their driving behavior from daytime driving to night driving and suffer the consequences for it. Night driving requires you to be as attentive as possible because anything can happen. Many drivers are tired and distracted when driving at night, and their own drowsiness can affect their driving. Night time drivers can be very unpredictable.

What are the negatives of night driving?

1. Less visibility
2. Processing surprise situations takes more time
3. Less reaction time creates longer stopping distances

I know many parents who are too afraid to practice with their teen at night because of these negatives, but our state requires the parent to give their teen ten hours of night driving practice before they test for their license. I think that's a good thing. Make sure to use your high beams if needed, but make sure you dim them when oncoming vehicles are about 500 feet away from you and also when you are approaching them 500 feet from the rear. You don't want your high beams to bounce off their rearview mirror into their eyes. If you have high beams from another vehicle bouncing off your rearview mirror into your own eyes, then use the dimmer switch on your rearview mirror, if you have one. It will decrease the glare. You can also focus on the right white line as a guide for a moment or two if the high beams from oncoming vehicles are affecting your ability to drive safely. Once the glare is gone, you can move your eyes back to the middle of the road.

Story Time

A few years ago, four college guys were coming home after a night out on the town when the driver fell asleep and hit the center median so hard that the car stalled in the middle of the road. When they got out of the car to push it to the right shoulder, two of the guys were struck by another vehicle because the driver couldn't see well enough in the dark until it was too late. One passenger had multiple broken bones and was paralyzed from the waist down, and the other passenger had multiple broken bones and a traumatic brain injury, with memory issues to this day. What started out as a fun night turned into a nightmare. It's so important that you look down the road as far as you can so there are no surprises. Drowsiness mixed with drinking during nighttime hours is a recipe for disaster.

A few tips for night driving:

1. Slow down. You'll need extra time to process and react to things.
2. Be extra careful on two-lane highways. Those vehicles tend to come very close to the yellow line.
3. Keep a safe distance behind the vehicle in front of you.
4. Don't drive tired.
5. Clean your headlights at least once a month so you have the most effective headlights possible when there is limited visibility.

The NHTSA reports that only 25 percent of all motor vehicle crashes occur at night, but approximately 50 percent of FATAL car crashes happen when it's dark, despite the fact that there are fewer drivers on the roads. Watch out for intoxicated drivers between 10:00 p.m. and 2:00 a.m., especially on the weekends. But if you take your time, constantly scan the road from left to right, and keep the distractions in your vehicle to a minimum, you'll do great!

37

Parents

Parents are interesting creatures. I'm still trying to figure them out. I'm a parent, and I'm still trying to figure myself out. Most of the parents I work with are great. Occasionally I get parents who just want to throw money at me to teach their teen to drive without any involvement themselves. I don't let that happen. Parents have to be involved in their teen's driving life. Parents are the true heroes in the situation. Raising kids to teenhood and then adulthood brings big changes, not only for you, but for your parents. They spend all those years pouring into you, only to have you move out at some point. Driving is a very important skill they want you to learn before that happens. They want to make sure you are fully confident and equipped to drive by yourself. Throughout the process, driving can be very emotional and personal, so you have to be as flexible and as level-headed as possible. It's a big deal to have a driver's license, and the state you live in only wants to give licenses to teens who will be mature and make wise decisions as a new driver. Is that you? I hope so.

Yes, there is a chance your parents will freak out a little bit when you drive together. Dad might yell and grab the "scream handle." Mom might keep hitting her fake brake. But remember, their hearts are in the right place, and they want the best for you. That's why they invested their lives in you. They clothe you, feed you, and give you a phone, etc., so give them a break, and try to empathize with those poor people. They probably worry about you and the decisions you will make more than you realize. If you've been an idiot and made poor choices in the past, then there's a good chance they'll be extra nervous about the choices you'll make after getting your driver's license. You understand that, don't you? If so, then now's the time to straighten up, make healthier choices, and strengthen the bridge you've done some damage to. The more they see your consistency in being trustworthy, the less they'll worry about you and the car.

Story Time

A sweet student of ours named Ashley lived outside of our driving area, so we had to meet up at a halfway point to start her lesson. Ashley was behind the wheel doing the driving when she and her mom entered the parking lot. I was happy that her mom was practicing with her. When Ashley got out of her mom's car and started walking toward our car, I noticed something was off. As her mom drove away, I noticed Ashley kept wiping her face. It turns out she had been crying. After pressing her for a minute, Ashley told me that her mom yelled at her for not changing lanes quickly enough. I felt bad for her, so we sat there for a minute or two so she could compose herself. We finally started driving, but within two minutes I heard her sniffling, so I glanced over at her and noticed the tears coming down her face. That was dangerous because the road was all blurry for her. After pulling over and attempting to regroup again, Ashley told me her mind wasn't in a good place and she wasn't able to continue the lesson. I did everything I could to pump her up, but nothing worked, so I drove her home and then headed back to the office. I contacted her mother later that day and had to tell Ashley's mom to work harder at keeping her cool.

A few tips for dealing with your parents:

1. Listen to their wisdom. They have good stuff to share.
2. You live under their roof, so keep your room clean and do your chores.
3. Show that you are responsible with the little things, and they'll begin to trust you with bigger things, like the car.
4. Be honest with them. They want to be there for you and help you.
5. They may be nervous teaching you to drive, so give them a break.

A few tips for parents dealing with teens:

1. Listen to your teens and their concerns about driving.
2. Keep encouraging them and celebrate their successes with them. Let them know when they do things well and when you've seen growth.

3. Maintain your composure and stay as level-headed as possible. Teens will feed off your energy, whether good or bad.
4. If you are feeling stressed, then suck on a lollipop, chew gum, or do anything that can help keep your jaw from tightening up. It helps many of our parents.

Perhaps take your teen out for a meal or dessert after your driving time together. It gives you both a chance to decompress and do away with any stress that was built up during your driving time. Lastly, remember that you are not just a team; you are family, and the driving investment you pour into your teen will pay off. You just have to get through the pain cave. Remember, you are creating lifelong memories together. Make them the best they can be with no regrets. You got this!

38
Parking Lots

Parking lots are a crazy world of their own. I'm serious. I don't like being in parking lots very much. Most drivers take parking lots for granted. But you really have to pay attention and keep those eyes moving because at times it seems like cars come out of nowhere. Many parking lots are poorly designed, and they never seem to look the same. The more parking lots you drive in, the more you'll scratch your head, wondering what the designers were thinking. Crashes in parking lots can happen at any time, so the slower you go, the more time you'll have to react to those boneheads who whip through the parking lot.

High school parking lots can also be crazy. We have a local high school that hasn't repaved their parking lot in well over ten years. I've heard of at least five fender benders over the years in that parking lot because the lines have faded so much that some of the teen drivers take their turns too tightly or too widely and dent bumpers.

When you are looking for a parking space, make sure you don't take your eyes off your driving for too long, because that could be right when a car backs out of a spot and hits you, or you take a turn too wide and crunch some nice sports car.

Story Time

One time I was sitting in a parking lot eating my burger, fries, and chocolate shake when a teen came out of the drive-through. He was looking down at his food and didn't see the cross traffic in the parking lot. He hit a car coming from his left to the right. Minor damage done, but it's just more proof that paying attention to your driving is more important than your chicken nuggets. I also saw someone almost back into a woman who was pushing her shopping cart down the parking lot aisle.

Parking lots can actually over-stimulate your senses. Just the other day my teen daughter and I went to the mall. The parking lot had slanted parking spaces so you could only drive down that aisle if you were heading in the same direction, but she missed it because of all the people walking in front and in back of her truck. Her brain was trying to process everything and didn't notice. She drove us the wrong direction and wasn't able to turn sharp enough into an open parking space, so she had to try again a couple of aisles down.

A few tips for driving in parking lots:

1. Keep scanning the parking lot ahead and to your right and left.

2. Be aware of the white back-up lights. It means a vehicle is backing out of a space.

3. When backing out of a space, make sure you don't back into someone else who is also backing out or trying to pass behind you.

4. If possible, pull forward into the parking space so that you can exit by driving forward. With so many SUVs and trucks these days, it's hard to see when backing a smaller vehicle out of a space.

5. If no cars are coming down the aisle toward you, try to drive down the middle of the aisle so you can respond quickly to people coming from your right and left—including runaway shopping carts.

6. Don't hit anyone or anything.

Practice driving in parking lots with your family. If you are a parent reading this, then let your teen drive when you run errands so they have a chance at maneuvering around the parking lots. In my experience, teens are weak in parking lots because they don't get enough experience. Parents and teens tell me it's scary practicing with real cars. Yes, it can be. But remember, practice makes progress!

39

Passengers

So you want to go out with your friends and drive around town having fun? Hold on to that thought for a moment, dude. I'm sure being the mature, wise teen you are, you'll want to do it safely and legally. It's great that you're going to have a license, a car to drive, your parents' trust, and a little money to have some fun, but you have to remember to do it safely.

Remember this: as the driver, you are the captain of your own ship. What you say goes, and your passengers have to do what you tell them, or they can get out of the car and walk home. Your number one priority is to get your passengers to each destination safely. That takes full cooperation from your passengers. They have to be cool and not put your lives at risk in any way.

I used to go out with my friends on the weekends and have a burger, fries, and a shake, and then head over to the movies or bowling alley. We had a blast. The one thing I always did was wear my seat belt. Perhaps I learned that from my own Driver's Ed class. But others in the car didn't. We used to blast the radio and yell and talk and laugh and were probably distracting our friend who was driving. Looking back on those days, I'm surprised we never crashed.

Did you know the more passengers you have in your vehicle, the more the risk of a crash goes up? According to AAA, adding just one teen passenger doubles the chances of a fatal crash, and with two or more teens in the car, the risk of a fatal crash can go up by a whopping 300 percent! What does that mean? It means that y'all are causing too much of a combined distraction to your driver, so you need to chill out and calm down. You're trusting your driver to get you to your fun, so help the dude actually get you there.

Story Time

After school one day, a 16-year-old girl was driving with her boyfriend beside her and two other couples packed in the backseat, unbuckled. She was speeding when her boyfriend jokingly yanked the steering wheel. She lost control of the car and crashed it, killing all four friends in the backseat. There were many bad links in the chain of events. Let's count them.

1. Overloaded backseat
2. No seat belts
3. She was speeding
4. Boyfriend yanked the steering wheel

As you can see, if one of those links didn't happen, then there is a good chance four people wouldn't have died that day. Just that story alone should stir something in you and motivate you to do the right thing when you drive or are a passenger. In an interview, the girl said that she had rules when she drove with her parents but no rules when driving with her friends. In the end, I'm sure she regretted her decision-making. Don't let what happened to them happen to you. Be a mature driver, and always do the right thing. It ain't worth it.

A few tips for passengers:

1. Don't be a distraction to your driver.
2. Wear your seat belt.
3. Don't block your driver's view. Keep your big head out of the way when needed.
4. Be a second set of eyes to help navigate and see potentially dangerous situations.

A few tips for the driver:

1. Make sure your passengers are all wearing seat belts.
2. Don't overload your car. Obey the law.
3. Don't allow yourself to get distracted.
4. Don't speed and put your passengers at risk.
5. Don't tailgate.

Both the driver and the passenger have to work together to make sure the drive time is safe and you get to your destination in one piece. Remember: the driver needs to be in charge and the passengers play the support role in the vehicle. The driver needs to understand how important his or her responsibility is when driving with passengers. Put the distractions aside, drive with plenty of rest, and don't be impaired in any way. Arrive alive!

40
Passing

Watch out! Passing can be a dangerous move. Passing other vehicles needs a plan and decisive action. Here in the United States, the rule is passing on the left, which is where faster traffic moves. Slower moving vehicles stay to the right. Passing cars is a skill that needs to be mastered or bad things can happen.

Story Time

I remember it like it was yesterday. It was Monday, November 1, 1982. The day after Halloween. Even though I was two weeks short of turning 15 years old and had no permit, my dad asked me if I wanted to drive. I jumped at the chance, since it was just a straight shot down the two-lane highway for 100 miles. We were traveling through the Mohave Desert from Mammoth Lakes to Los Angeles. The old, brown station wagon didn't have much power but was fun to drive. My dad cracked open a beer and chugged it down in about five minutes. Then he cracked open a *second* beer and chugged that one down in about seven minutes. He closed his eyes and took a nap. Yeah, everything about that was illegal, but that was my dad for you. About twenty minutes into the drive, I came upon a slower car on the two-lane highway. My dad felt me slow down and opened his eyes. He told me I could go ahead and pass the car when no oncoming traffic was coming. I looked and saw my opportunity to move into the oncoming traffic lane and felt good about the clearance. The problem was, the car didn't have enough power to make the pass quickly enough. As I was trying to pass, I suddenly saw a car appear from over a hill, and I knew I had to really speed up. My dad suddenly got much more interested in the situation. He told me to go faster, then repeated himself again, and a third time, with his voice a little louder each time. I pushed the gas pedal all the way to the floor. We were closing in on each other, me and the oncoming car, each going at least 70 miles per hour. The oncoming car flashed his high beams at me. As I moved even with the car next to me, I wondered why he wasn't slowing down for me to pass him up. Being so young, I was immediately feeling overwhelmed, with a lot going through my mind in those short moments. Suddenly, the station wagon's power kicked in, and I flew past the car on my right and quickly moved over in front of him—just in time—as the other car flew past with his horn blasting. Amen! No one died that day. My dad just shook his head, and I wiped my sweaty hands on my pants and kept driving.

A few tips for passing on a two-lane road:

1. Stay back a good distance behind the vehicle you want to pass.
2. Get momentum by speeding up.
3. Put your left signal/blinker/indicator on before you move left.
4. On a two-lane road, check the oncoming traffic lane to make sure vehicles are not coming at you.
5. Look over your left shoulder to make sure you are not being passed.
6. Safely change lanes and make the pass without going over the speed limit.
7. Once you pass the vehicle, return to your lane as soon as possible, but give enough space to the car you passed. Three seconds in front of them is a good distance.
8. Only pass one car at a time on a two-lane highway. It's too dangerous to hang out in the other lane for too long with traffic coming toward you. Don't die!

There's no need to go over the posted speed limit and break the law just to pass another vehicle. It's perfectly all right to drive a couple of ticks under the speed limit. Stay relaxed and enjoy your ride. The main point is to arrive to your destination in one piece.

41
Pedestrians

Watch out for people! They only have one life, and if you run into them, then perhaps that's the end of that story. According to the Governors Highway Safety Association, pedestrian deaths have increased over the last few years, averaging well over 7,000 pedestrian deaths a year. That's over twenty people killed by vehicles each day! What the heck? That's almost one death per hour. The majority of those deaths were children and older adults. I'm assuming that's because older adults and children aren't quite as aware of an idiot driver coming and might not move as quickly out of the way. According to the NHTSA, a pedestrian is injured every eight minutes. That's crazy! The Department of Transportation reported that in one year, a whopping 67,000 people walking, running or standing were involved in a collision with a vehicle and required a trip to the hospital. It's obvious you need to pay attention on the road. As you've probably noticed, paying attention is the theme of driving and the theme of this book.

Kids run out into the street. They ride their bikes down driveways into the street. They chase the ball into the street, so it's very important that you keep moving your eyes left to right while driving. Even joggers think they can dart out in front of your car with plenty of room to get across the street, only to slip on a wet road or trip on their own shoelace. Gosh, can you imagine someone dying because they tripped on their own shoelace while running across traffic? I'm sure it's happened somewhere.

Story Time

A woman in Nashville stepped off the curb into the crosswalk on her green light. Just then, a car turning left entered the crosswalk and struck her. She lived but had bruises and a torn tendon in her foot. The driver of the car that struck her was looking down the road for clearance before turning left at the intersection. His eyes weren't looking at anyone on the corner about to step down into the crosswalk area. She had walked just a few feet into the street when he struck her.

This woman was very lucky, but it's the story of hundreds of pedestrians each year. That's why it's so important to keep your eyes moving, especially in areas where there are crosswalks.

Another Story

One time when I was 19 years old, after I had purchased Sean's convertible, I was driving late at night through a town called

Lone Pine in California. The cop had been behind me for the past six miles or so. As I entered downtown Lone Pine, I happened to look in my rearview mirror to see the cop still behind me just as the only pedestrian in the entire town stepped off the curb into the crosswalk. When I looked back to the road, he was already seven or eight feet into the crosswalk, and I decided to drive to the left around him. The pedestrian obviously stopped for me since my car was bigger than he was. After going around the guy, I saw the police car lights go on, and the cop immediately pulled me over. He asked me why I didn't stop for the pedestrian, and I told him I didn't see the guy because I was looking in my mirror at that exact moment. The officer gave me a ticket for failing to yield to a pedestrian in a crosswalk. I had to pay a fine and a lot of money to attend an eight-hour traffic school class to get those points off my record. So don't do that. Always yield to anyone walking, jogging or biking.

A few tips about pedestrians:

1. At intersections, make sure to stay behind the crosswalk lines when turning right.

2. When turning left, scan the crosswalk to your left to make sure people aren't entering it from either corner to cross in front of you.

3. Watch out to your right for people stepping out between the parked cars to jaywalk illegally in front of you or to simply get to the driver's side of their parked car.

4. Yield to pedestrians as soon as they step off the curb.

5. Always yield to pedestrians on the sidewalk when you are turning right into a driveway, alley or a public parking garage.
6. You must yield to all pedestrians in a school zone or crosswalk when the yellow lights are flashing.

Make sure you have enough insurance to cover any injuries you cause to a pedestrian. Better yet, just don't hit them. The more you scan, the more you can process, and the better chance you have to respond to any pedestrians.

42
Permit Test

In my opinion, the permit test is the hardest part of the entire driving process. The permit test is the written test you take to get your learner's permit. No driving involved! It's the very first thing you do before entering the driving world. In most states, it's a multiple-choice test you take on a computer. It's thirty questions here in Tennessee, and if you miss too many, the test shuts off without letting you continue. It sounds kind of cruel, huh? Tennessee now gives teens the option to take the permit test online in the comfort of their own homes. Perhaps that's so the DMV employees don't have to see any more distraught and crying teens.

    The best way for you to study and pass the permit test on your first attempt is to have your parents study with you and drill you on everything. In my experience, many of the teens I work with miss the questions that ask for numbers.

Example: What's the legal blood alcohol concentration level for someone twenty-one years or older? The options might be .08 or .008 or .8. The driving manual in our state says .08, but if you are nervous, then you might get a foggy brain and miss the answer. Study very hard, and have your parents help you break down any lingo you don't know the definition of. Go to your local DMV office and obtain the state driving manual to help you study.

A few topics you might be tested on:

1. Road signs and lines
2. Basic speed laws in different areas
3. Alcohol and drugs
4. Stopping distances from stop line, railroad tracks, fire hydrants, etc.

If you have test anxiety, then do whatever you can to get your "Zen" on and relax. Some people are not good test-takers, but don't psych yourself out before you even arrive to take the test. Remember, if it's a multiple-choice test, the answers are right in front of you. Simply use process of elimination and get rid of the most obvious wrong answers. However, if you take a Driver's Ed course and study the driving manual, you have a better chance of doing well. In our state, teens are allowed to test for their permit before taking Driver's Ed, but with a Driver's Ed class under your belt, you might walk in there with more confidence. Whatever works for you.

Story Time

A couple of years ago, a mom called me and told me her son failed the permit test four times, and she didn't know what to do to help him. She was going crazy taking him back to retest over and over. I asked her if she had ever studied with him to help him. She told me she hadn't because she believed it was his responsibility to study on his own since it was going to be his permit. I told her if she studied with him, she could break down phrases like "implied consent law" and "graduated licensing program" to help him understand their meanings in case he missed questions on those topics. If she studied with him, he increased his chances of passing next time around, and she would have her sanity back. She reluctantly agreed. I gave her information about our upcoming classes, and she appeared interested, but I never heard back from her. Oh well.

    Just make sure you study for the test and ask your family for help. You got this! You're a smart person. Always dwell on your successes in life. Do you know how to tie your shoes? Do you know how to pet the dog? If you answered yes to both of those questions, then you are on your way. Put a study plan in place, dive into that driving manual, and go for it!

43
Relationships

Most people don't understand how relationships can affect a person's driving. There are so many dynamics and types of relationships between people. Think about what you are like when you're in the car with different friends or certain family members. Do you always act the same way? Are you quiet and focused when driving with your friends? What about when driving with your dad? Many teens admit that they drive differently according to who's in the vehicle with them. They drive a certain way with mom in the car and another way with their best friend in the car. The attitude changes, but the new young driver rarely notices it. Perhaps a teen guy is driving with a buddy he looks up to, and his buddy doesn't want to wear a seat belt. The driver might not feel confident enough to speak up, because he doesn't want anything negative to come out of it. He might even bow down to the silent peer pressure and not wear his own seat belt. Or he'll speed up over the speed limit if the other guy tells him to.

How about the dating relationship? Do you both argue while driving? Do the conversations get deep? The level of distracted driving can differ depending upon the type of relationship you have with your passengers. Perhaps your friends want to blast the music (which is very distracting), or perhaps your mom likes to catch up on life and do mommy/daughter time together.

You have to remember that you are the captain of your own ship, and your passengers have to be cool and go with the flow when you are driving. The driver is the most important person in the car, followed by young children, because they are the most vulnerable and usually unaware of the dangers around them when the vehicle is moving.

Story Time

It was prom night, and a young, high school couple started the evening out on the right note—prom pictures, dinner, dancing—but then the drama came. They got into some sort of argument at the dance, and it continued in the car on the way home from the big night. The boyfriend got emotional and decided to speed to scare his girl. He crashed the car and killed both of them.

With certain relationships come certain emotions. That's why it's so important to check yourself and concentrate on the drive. Perhaps you and your dad butt heads when he lets you do the driving, and it affects HOW you drive. He might make you nervous because he's nervous. Perhaps your mom thinks she knows it all and wants you to drive her way rather than the safest way.

A few tips for driving and relationships:

1. Maintain your concentration while driving.
2. Don't let your friends peer pressure you.
3. Don't get caught up in deep conversations.
4. Don't let your emotions take over.
5. Just because you respect and look up to your passenger, it doesn't mean they can influence you to drive risky.

Remember to be the same responsible driver no matter who's in the vehicle with you. You are your own driver and know the law. You know how to do the right thing. Go for it!

44
Right-of-Way

The right-of-way (or yield) laws help people understand who goes first at an intersection, in parking lots, or at areas of merging. The problem is that many licensed drivers either don't know the law, forgot the law, or don't care about the law. Never assume the other driver will give you your right-of-way.

You must give the right of way when:

1. The other driver gets to the four-way stop intersection before you.
2. The other driver is on your right if you get to the intersection at the same time.
3. You want to enter a roundabout but are not in it yet.
4. You are merging onto a highway or a freeway and still on the on-ramp.

5. You are waiting to make or finish a left turn on a green, yellow, or red light with oncoming traffic entering the intersection.
6. You are waiting to make a right turn, and traffic is going straight coming from your left.
7. You are waiting to make a left turn on highways with non-stop cross traffic.
8. There are blinking red lights. You have to come to a complete stop first, then yield to cross traffic.

Story Time

A young woman was approaching a four-way intersection with a flashing red light. She stopped at the flashing red as was required by law, but then she proceeded to go through the intersection instead of giving the right-of-way to the car coming from her left on a blinking yellow. The other car T-boned her, and she died. She didn't understand the right-of-way law. The flashing yellow light for the other driver indicated he was to proceed with caution, but he didn't think that the young woman would pull out in front of him. She was responsible for her own death.

Knowing right-of-way laws and obeying them will keep you safe and will decrease the chances of a crash. Stay alert out there, and keep scanning the road left to right so you can process things quickly. Sounds like the theme of this book doesn't it? Yep!

45
Road Rage

Ahh yes. Road rage, the cousin of aggressive driving. The two best friends who love to hang out and talk all things anger, impatience, and revenge. Over the years, I've learned that aggressive driving can turn into road rage. The question is: why do so many people drive aggressively? Here are some of the answers I've received in our traffic school classes:

1. I'm always running late.
2. I don't have time for stupid drivers.
3. I have a low patience level.
4. I need to be in front of other cars with open road ahead of me.

Recently I had a young adult tell me he got a ticket driving 127 miles per hour in a 70-speed zone. He got a huge ticket, two weeks of community service, and had to come to me for a four-hour class. I was shocked to learn the judge did NOT suspend his license. Go figure.

Another way aggressive driving can easily turn into road rage is when a second driver doesn't like what the aggressive driver is doing. Sometimes the second driver can involve themselves in something that has nothing to do with them. Other times the second driver is being tailgated or cut off by an aggressive driver, and then a bad situation arises.

Just quote Forrest Gump: "Life is like a bunch of chocolates. You never know what you're gonna get." Well, drivers are like a bunch of chocolates. You never know what you're gonna get! That's why it's important to stay away from drama out on the roads. You don't know what a person's history is five minutes before they got behind the wheel and crossed paths with you. Be the better person!

Story Time

I had a former student post on his social media that he likes braking really hard in front of drivers to watch their reactions in his rearview mirror. It did something inside of him—gave him some sort of joy or rush to do that to others. It's very dangerous to brake-check other drivers, so I called him to tell him not to do that. He didn't pick up his phone, so I told him to call me back or I was going to call his mom to tell her what he was doing with her minivan. Sure enough, no returned call. So I called his mom, let her know, and she ended up taking the minivan away from him for three months. Ha! I ran into him at a school play a few months later, and he made a face at me when I approached him. He wasn't willing to take responsibility for his illegal and dangerous behavior and was mad at me for telling his mom. I guess he didn't learn his lesson.

Another Story

A driver cut off another driver, and the second driver retaliated by cutting off the first driver. They yelled at each other at the red light and flipped the middle finger at each other. The vengeful driver followed the other driver to his neighborhood and noted where he lived. A week later, he hid in the bushes with a gun to shoot him when he came out. He waited a few hours, and in the dark night, a man came outside and got into his car. The vengeful driver ran up to him and shot him two times. Turns out, he shot the wrong guy! He shot the twenty-year-old son, instead. Fortunately, the son lived! The vengeful driver went to prison.

A few examples of how road rage can occur:

1. The driver was already angry about something when he got behind the wheel.
2. The driver has a high opinion of himself and doesn't care about other drivers.
3. The driver has a short fuse, and you end up setting their emotional bomb off by simply going too slow in front of them or anything else he doesn't like.
4. The driver knows the police aren't around, so he can take revenge on you for something he perceives you did wrong to him without being caught.

A few tips to help you deal with road-ragers:

1. Don't engage them. Wave to them and smile.
2. Throw up the peace sign. Yes, it still works in the USA. I've used it and I still get a friendly response.
3. You can try to ignore them if you feel like it, but some drivers don't want to be ignored; they want to be acknowledged. So say you are sorry, even if it's not your fault. Defuse the situation and get them out of your life.
4. Remember, you don't know that other driver, so don't take things personally and get involved with them.

A few tips to not become a road-rager:

1. Be kind to other people. If you behave kindly to others, then it might carry over into the car.
2. Don't take bad drivers personally. You don't know each other. Let it go.
3. Be the hero on the road. When getting behind the wheel, say a prayer or do a self-check— anything to help keep your cool.
4. Go to some anger management classes to help find the root of your anger.

In my humble opinion, road rage is a sociological disease. It can even be passed down from parent to teen. We tend to emulate the most important influences in our life. If an athlete becomes a coach, he might coach with the same style that he was coached. Teen drivers watch their parents drive, pick up on some of the same habits and attach them to their own driving style—even aggressive driving and road rage. It's scary! Road rage is bad for everyone. You don't want that reputation, and you certainly don't want anything bad to happen if you lose your temper. Just let it go.

46
Road Trips

I love road trips! I've travelled from Florida to Washington State, up and down California, and all over the mid-south. I've been on many mission trips and white-water rafting trips with friends and created some great memories and good friendships over the decades. Fortunately, we've never had flat tires, engine trouble, or anything that would damper our experiences. I guess I'm one of the few lucky ones.

I'm usually a very simple road-tripper. I get my bottled water and my snacks, and I'm ready to go. However, it takes a little more than that to make sure my road trip is safe. If you use wisdom when headed out for a road trip, you'll save yourself a lot of headaches and possible dangerous situations.

Story Time

One time while driving through some back roads of Oregon, I saw what looked like a group of albino cows – I had never seen all white cows before, and they intrigued me, so I pulled the rental car off the road to take a photo. After a quick picture and conversation with one cow, I got back into the car and tried to pull back onto the road. I quickly realized I had stopped the car in very loose soil that started to sink the car. Sure enough, my back tires got stuck, and it took me two hours to flag a car down, have them call a tow truck in the next town, and wait for the tow truck to show up, only for it to take them five minutes to pull my car forward ten feet. I was really frustrated at myself for not watching where I was parking. Luckily, I've never had anything worse than that happen on a road trip. Just watch out, make a plan, and you'll do great!

A few tips for a successful road trip:

1. Take your car to a shop to have the oil and all fluids checked and replenished, if needed.
2. Have the shop check your tires and belts to see if they need to be replaced.
3. Make sure to get plenty of rest before you head out on your trip. Many drivers spend so much time preparing that their brains can't turn off, and they end up tired at the start.
4. Try to drive during your normal "waking" hours so your body can handle the drive.
5. Take a break every 100 miles to stretch, eat, and refresh yourself.
6. Make your "time good" rather than trying to make "good time."

7. Don't be aggressive and get frustrated with other drivers. Forgive and drive on. It's tough to drive when you are frustrated and stressed, and it drives your passengers crazy.

8. Plan your route ahead of time so you know where you are headed and don't get lost.

9. Don't drive more than eight hours a day, which equals about 500 miles. If you can switch drivers, then that is a plus. Splitting the driving up helps you rest and regain your senses.

10. Stop and take some photos of unique places and things you might not see again. It helps to create memories when looking back years later.

There are probably more tips I could mention, but just use your brain and don't be an idiot on your road trip. Road trips can be fun and educational and can create a lot of cool memories. Don't rush the road trip like a lot of dads do. Make the road trip fun. Take your time, learn about some of the towns you might be traveling through, and give yourself an awesome experience and memories of a great time.

47
School Buses

Since school buses are carrying kids, it's important that we look out for them. According to the NHTSA, buses have been around since 1915. In 1939, the color yellow was adopted for national use. That's a cool fact you can share with your family. School buses help a lot of families because many kids can't get a ride to school. According to School Bus Fleet, there are over 479,000 buses providing transportation to students each day in the United States. That's a lot of yellow! They also say that over 25 million children are riding those buses. And more than half of the students in grades K-12 use the bus to get to school.

I hear stories and read stories about vehicles going around school buses or not stopping for buses when required. So let's go over this. In most states, drivers are required to stop in all directions when a school bus has stopped and put the red flashing lights on with the stop arm extended. If you are behind a school bus, then you might need to stay back at least twenty-five feet. Wait for the students to get off the bus, because some of them may need to cross the street. You are not required to stop if a school bus is coming in your direction on the other side of a physical median or barrier.

Story Time

Two twin six-year-old brothers, their nine-year-old sister, and another friend were struck by a 24-year-old woman while they were crossing the two-lane highway to get on the morning school bus. The bus driver had the stop arm extended and the red lights flashing. The siblings died and their friend lived. How crushing that is for the parents to lose all three children. The driver simply was not paying enough attention.

A few tips about school buses:

1. Yellow flashing lights are a warning for drivers that the bus is slowing down to stop.
2. Red flashing lights mean drivers should stop completely.
3. Wait for children to exit the bus and either walk up onto the sidewalk or around the front of the bus and across the street in front of your vehicle.
4. Wait for lights to stop flashing and the stop arm to fully retract.
5. Double-check that children are cleared out of the street, and then drive on.

According to the National Association of State Directors of Pupil Transportation Services (that's a long name!), during a one-day survey of 34 states, almost 52,000 vehicles illegally passed up school buses when the stop arm was extended on a single school day during the 2020-2021 school year. That's crazy! How can drivers not see the need to stop? Since only 34 states had made the reports, I'm sure that number is actually much higher. Also, like in the story above, many kids are killed crossing the street to or from the school bus. Even though the bus driver had the flashing red lights on and the stop arm extended, the drivers simply were not paying enough attention to the situation.

We must protect our students at bus stops, in school zones, and at their houses waiting for the school bus. Pay attention, scan left to right, slow down, and stop when necessary. That way, everyone can have a future on this planet.

48
School Zones

Here's the deal with school zones: they require all of our attention. If you are not paying attention while driving in a school zone, then people can get injured…or worse. During certain hours of the day, a school zone will be active with yellow blinking lights and a lower speed limit. You'll usually see them about a block before the actual school crosswalk. In our area, school zones are usually 15 or 20 miles per hour. Just make sure you are at the required speed right where the new speed limit sign is posted. Remember, most drivers are passive drivers and might not notice the speed change or the flashing yellow lights until it's too late.

Many school zones have a crossing guard directing traffic, but you should still keep your eyes moving, because the crossing guard has a lot going on and can't see everything. The crossing guard is multi-tasking, trying to help students, buses and vehicles get through the school zone and in and out of crosswalks, so be patient. Our state has averaged over 1,000 car crashes in school zones each year since 2016. That's a lot of crashes, considering students are out of school on weekends and summer and holiday breaks.

Story Time

A mom picked up her daughter, walked across the school zone crosswalk and, along with the crossing guard, was struck by a car. The car was speeding through the school zone and not paying attention. The little girl died. That is a horrible story to have to share. Stuff like that wouldn't happen if people are paying attention.

A few tips for driving in a school zone:

1. Slow down and obey the school zone speed limit.
2. Keep scanning left to right and as far ahead as possible.
3. Try to look through the windshield of the vehicle in front of you to see what they see.
4. Stay off your phone and remain focused on your surroundings.

Automobile Association of America reports that 34 percent of Tennessee drivers admit to speeding in active school zones, and a whopping 26 percent admitted to being on their cell phones while driving through active school zones.

The next time you drive through a school zone, remember all the tips I gave you, and be aware of all that is going on.

49

Seat Belts

You all know what a seat belt is and most likely wore one today. Every state has a seat belt law, and it's required that you wear seat belts properly. Go out to your family vehicle and check them out. As a kid I remember seeing the seat belts in our cars, but we weren't told to put them on. I think most parents back in the '70s didn't care about using them. The seat belts in our cars only had the lap portion, with nothing over the shoulder. I noticed our '80s cars had added shoulder restraints with the lap belt for more protection. Once I reached twelfth grade, for some reason my buddy Bill and I decided to wear our seat belts and would constantly remind each other at the same time by saying out loud, "Safety first!" It was silly, but it worked. I noticed most teens would arrive and leave school without seat belts on.

Currently, the national use of seat belts is about 90 percent. I scratch my head every time I see a driver without a seat belt on. It takes about two seconds to grab it and click it. Do it, or you'll regret losing your gorgeous teeth when you hit the airbag, dashboard, or windshield.

Story Time

A dad I know bought his beautiful, bright yellow, dream Ford Mustang. He refused to buckle up, even after his teen daughter argued with him many times about it. The dad paid for his daughter to attend our classes and was taught by me to wear her seat belt. Well, the dad was caught up in a crash on a rainy day on the freeway, and even though the crash wasn't his fault, he almost died because he had no seat belt on and went through the windshield. When he came up out of his seat toward the windshield, his femur was broken by the bottom of the steering wheel. Check that visual out. Sorry, not sorry.

His wife emailed me some of the gruesome photos of him in the hospital with a shaved head and staples and stitches everywhere. His wife was injured as well, but I can't remember if she had buckled up. A few months later, I was at a burger joint when I saw both parents walking from the parking lot into the restaurant. They were both limping five months later! It broke my heart. So what's the lesson here? Wear your seat belt! Seat belts working together with airbags is the safest you can get.

A few of the lame excuses for not wearing a seat belt are:

1. It's uncomfortable.
2. I forgot.

3. I'm only driving a short distance from the house to fast food.

4. I'll take my chances.

I've had teens tell me that seat belts can also kill a person, but no one has ever given me a good statistic to convince me that it's more dangerous to wear one. You have to wear them properly for them to be effective. Don't have any slack in your belt. Keep your butt on the seat and your feet on the car floor, and you should be good to go.

One former student of mine told me that she and her friend were driving down the friend's dirt driveway when he decided to be silly with the steering wheel, turning it back and forth. Well, he lost control and rolled the pick-up truck down the embankment. Neither one of them had their seat belts on, and both windows were rolled down. They both could have been ejected and crushed to death. That didn't happen. Both got bruised up, though. Fortunately, they weren't injured any worse. Get that visual? So dude, do the wrong thing and possibly die. It will be very inconvenient for your loved ones, right?

A few tips about seat belts:

1. Wear your seat belt properly, which is over the shoulder, across your chest, and over the hips. Don't wear the lap portion riding up over your stomach. Try to put the seat belt under a belt buckle, if you have one. That way it won't ride up over your hips.

2. Don't put the shoulder belt under your arm or behind your back. You will be defeating the purpose of that

part and could slam your face into the airbag or steering wheel.

3. Adjust your seat so the shoulder portion isn't rubbing up against your neck. Some cars have a tab that can adjust the height of the shoulder belt. Check it out in your vehicle.

4. Don't be lazy and lie down in the backseat with the belt off for a road trip. Always keep it on and wear it properly. Better to be safe than dead or injured, right?

5. Airbags working together with seat belts is the safest you can get.

6. Insist that all your passengers wear their seat belts. Remember, you are the captain of your ship. If they aren't wearing them, they can get slammed into you, and you can knock heads during a crash. Splattered brains are not a good look, except on Halloween.

That's a lot of tips. Just be cool and obey the law. It's there for your protection. Even with 90 percent of drivers wearing seat belts, we still have that 10 percent who don't care enough. Then they get hurt or killed, and we feel guilty about it—even if the crash wasn't our fault. Just do the right thing and protect your life…and theirs.

50

Signs and Lines

One of the most important parts of driving is learning the meaning of the signs and lines on the road. Signs and lines direct us and help us to drive in a safe manner to avoid crashes.

Signs

Road signs are those metal boards you see on the side of the road to warn drivers about potential hazards or situations, to help regulate the flow of traffic, or to give information.

Categories of Signs:

1. Regulatory signs—they have the red, white, or black background colors and are mostly speed limit signs, one-way signs, and stop signs. They help to regulate traffic.

2. Warning signs—these signs have a yellow or orange background color and are usually seen in construction zones. They are warning drivers of upcoming hazards or situations.

3. Guide and service signs—these have blue, brown, and green background colors. Blue signs could be hospitals or gas stations. Brown signs are often for historical landmarks or campgrounds. Green signs are destination signs telling you how far to the next exit.

Lines

Traffic lines keep everything going in a nice, orderly fashion. Yellow lines mean there is two-way traffic moving in opposite directions, so watch out that you don't drive on the wrong side of the street into oncoming traffic. White lines mean that traffic is moving in the same direction. You'll understand more by driving on the roads than you ever will by reading this chapter, so I won't go into a ton of detail, or your head will spin.

A few tips about road lines:

1. Yellow lines mean lanes move in opposite directions.

2. White solid lines mean lanes move in the same direction and to stay in the lane.

3. Broken white lines mean the same direction, but you can change lanes.

4. Double double-yellow lines mean to treat it like a median or an island of cement. Don't cross over them like I did.

Story Time

When I was 19 years old, I drove my white convertible down to visit my buddies at San Diego State University. I made a left turn over a double double-yellow line into the dormitory parking lot and found myself face-to-face with a cop. He gave me a ticket, and I ended up having to find an eight-hour traffic school class. I wasn't paying attention to the lines on the road and ended up paying big-time for it. Getting that one ticket cost me a couple hours in traffic court, a sizable fine over one hundred dollars, and an eight-hour traffic school class that cost about seventy-five dollars. We didn't have the internet back then, so I had to find a class in the phone book and find out how to actually get to the classroom in a different city from where I lived. It was a pain in the butt every way you look at it.

It's very important that you pay attention to all the signs and lines, because they are there to help you understand what the speed limit is, what might be coming up ahead, and where to go and not to go. Pay attention, obey the law, and you'll stay out of trouble.

51
Speeding

Let's face it: the faster the speed, the bigger the mess. We all understand that, yet so many of us continue to put lives at risk. In the '90s, California was debating increasing the freeway speed limit from 55 to 65 miles per hour. I seem to remember one opinion newspaper article read: "We realize speeding is dangerous, now get out of our way." I actually thought the writer was reading my young mind.

We have speed limits for a reason, and these days I usually agree with the speed limit signs. Sometimes I think the speed limit is a little too fast, and in other places I think it's too slow, but I'm still required to obey the law, regardless of how I feel about it. I think the big question of the day is: why do drivers speed? I've asked that question a ton of times over the years, and many of our adult and teen students have given answers.

Why Drivers Speed:

1. "I'm trying to make good time!"
2. "Come on, Bro, I'm not good at time management."
3. "I'm a very impatient person!"
4. "I'm not the problem! You're the problem! You're driving too slow!"
5. "Cops won't pull anyone over unless you're going seven miles per hour over."

Even in the car on a lesson the other day, I had a 15-year-old dude go over the speed limit at least ten times. In his particular case, he simply wasn't paying enough attention and hadn't developed the habit of glancing at his speedometer every five seconds. Yes, every five seconds.

Who's more likely to speed, men or women? The studies show that men speed more than women. One Canadian study says that male drivers between 15 and 35 years old make up 89 percent of extreme speeders.

The average driver is a selfish driver. Sorry, that's just a fact. We are in our own little world and drive very passively, only worrying about getting to our destination on our terms. The solution is getting out of ourselves and being more intentional as humans. The more intentional you are as a person, the more intentional you'll be as a driver. You have to live in the moment and truly be involved as much as you can with what is going on around you.

Story Time

A 16-year-old teen in Canada received over $1,100 in fines for driving 105 miles per hour and driving without a supervising driver. I guess he only had a permit. When asked why he was driving so fast, he told the officer that he had eaten too many hot wings and was rushing to use the bathroom with a colonic emergency. Not cool, dude!

I had a guy come to our traffic school class for speeding three times in less than three years. He told me he simply likes to speed. I reminded him of how dangerous it was and how much time and money he was giving up, but he just shrugged. Idiot.

Another Story

A 22-year-old in our traffic school class got a ticket driving 120 miles per hour in a 70-speed zone. His excuse was he had borrowed his mom's Chevy Corvette and didn't realize how fast he was going. I asked him if he didn't realize he was almost rear-ending everyone he had to go around on the freeway. He said no. Geez! The judge gave him two weeks of working for Habitat for Humanity building houses and put him on probation for six months. However, the judge did not suspend his license. Unbelievable!

I can share more stories with you that might take up this entire book. The bottom line is that innocent people die every day in this country because of selfish people not thinking about anyone else but themselves. It's ridiculous and wrong. You have no idea what will happen if you speed. It can catch up with you. The one day you decide to go five over the speed limit might be the same day a couple of kids enter the crosswalk and you can't stop in time. Get it? So slow down and be cool.

A few tips to help you not be an idiot speeder:

1. Check the side of the road for the speed limit sign.
2. Check your speedometer every five seconds. It's just a quick glance.
3. Go with the flow of traffic ONLY if it's at the speed limit or below. Don't be a law-breaker along with the other law-breakers. You'll be adding to the problem.
4. Tell yourself you'd rather be a hero than a zero and prove it by driving safe.

A few speeding facts for you:

1. When you speed, you lose vital stopping distance.
2. When you speed, you lose the ability to process things quickly enough.
3. When you speed, you lose necessary reaction time.
4. When you speed, your odds of a crash, injury, or death go up.
5. When you speed, you give away your hard-earned money in fines, fees, and time.

So don't be an idiot. When you speed, you are putting lives at risk, so chill out. Don't have a heavy foot or a big ego. Stay safe!

52

Stupidity

By this time, I'm sure you know the difference between right and wrong. Don't be a dork and do the wrong things when you are the driver or the passenger in a vehicle. Here's a list of some stupid and wrong things you could do:

1. Speeding
2. Impaired driving in any form
3. Aggressive driving
4. Road rage
5. Not wearing a seat belt
6. Driving with feet up on the dashboard
7. Overloading your vehicle with too many passengers
8. Distracted driving, like eating, phone use, putting on make-up, etc.

9. Drag-racing

10. Trying to beat a train

11. Passing in no-passing zones

12. Breaking any laws just to get home on time for curfew

13. Littering out your window

14. Not maintaining your vehicle—oil changes, checking tire tread, etc.

15. Sneaking out and not obeying your family rules

16. Flipping people off. They might follow you home.

17. Blasting your radio so you can't hear what's going on around you

18. Forgetting to pick Grandma up and to take her to lunch

19. Taking the car without asking your parents

I'm sure there's more. Feel free to add to the list. I wish someone had given me a list like this when I was a new driver. Perhaps I wasn't mature enough to even care about a list, though. Like I said before, if you spend all your time doing the right things as a driver or passenger, you won't have time to do the wrong things. I'm sure you are a smart person. You have a brain! You have every opportunity to make the best, healthiest, and wisest decisions when they come your way. Don't be a dork. Make yourself and your parents proud.

53
Traffic Court

So you got the ticket. I told you to slow down just a few chapters back! OK, so no one was hurt, but the ticket tells you what date to show up to court. What does that mean? When you go to traffic court, you'll be with a bunch of other lawbreakers who have to leave work or school to make an appearance in front of the judge. It stinks. Make sure you have the money to pay for your fine that day, if required. You could be there for a couple of hours until your name is called, and then you have to talk to the judge for a minute or two, explaining what you did. I've been to traffic court myself and have also sat in traffic court watching others speak with the judge. In one court I sat in, the judge gave the people a chance to say whether they were guilty, not guilty, or guilty with an explanation. Those who said they were guilty with an explanation went to the back of the line and waited for their chance to try to persuade the judge they were justified to have done what they did.

Traffic School

Sometimes the judge would let the driver off the hook after hearing their story. Other times she would assign them to take either a four-hour or an eight-hour Traffic School class, depending on how bad the driving infraction was. Usually speeding, running red lights, or running stop signs are good for a four-hour class. Drunk driving and multiple driving violations usually earns the driver an eight-hour class. I've had people in our class who received tickets for being on their phones. I'm glad law enforcement is cracking down on phone users. It sends a message that distracted driving is dangerous.

If they send you to traffic school, then you can pay about sixty dollars for a four-hour class and work those points off your record to avoid an insurance premium hike. In our traffic school, it's funny how so many drivers claim they didn't do anything wrong, or the cop was picking on them, or that everyone else is an idiot except them. I have heard every excuse in the book, and I just laugh to myself.

Story Time

I got a ticket way back in the late '90s for speeding at night, in the rain, in a construction zone and had to spend time in traffic court, pay a fine, and then attend a four-hour traffic school class with a huge fee. The judge was nice, but I couldn't understand how she could hold court a few times each week listening to people try to convince her it was a speed trap, or the cop pulled the wrong car over, or many cars were also speeding.

A few tips for traffic court:

1. Dress appropriately for court.
2. Bring enough money to pay for fines.
3. Be nice to the judge and the court clerk.
4. Don't get any more tickets.

I would say getting a speeding ticket cost me a total of about $225, and about seven or eight hours of my time traveling to court and traffic school. I finally came to my senses and slowed down. It wasn't worth losing all that time and money.

The traffic school class I teach these days is similar to the class I had to go to all those years ago.

Subjects we teach:

1. Speeding
2. Drunk driving
3. Aggressive driving
4. Distracted driving

There are more topics we can teach on, but we only have four hours to teach, so we have to hit the main topics that most drivers engage in.

Do yourself a favor: obey the law. Stay out of trouble, and you won't have to give up your time or your hard-earned money.

54
Traffic Lights

Hey dudes and dudettes, this is a topic that I am very passionate about because I have been in a couple of car crashes at traffic lights. I've been bumped in the back a couple of times with minimal damage but with time in the shop for repairs. Fortunately, the other drivers paid the bills. There are so many things happening at intersections that you have to be aware and on your game at all times.

Traffic lights have been around for over one hundred years to help regulate traffic and give vehicles moving in different directions a chance to get through intersections safely. There are three main colors of traffic lights: green, amber/yellow, and red. There are also blinking reds and yellows, as well as arrows. I'm sure you've seen them.

Pay attention as you approach an intersection because all light sequences aren't the same. Many traffic lights are on a timer at different times of the day or night, depending on how heavy or light the traffic. The majority of drivers are pretty impatient and don't like waiting at red lights. They often run red lights or go way over the speed limit to make sure they don't get stuck at the upcoming red light. But remember, any vehicle entering the intersection after the light has turned red is in violation of the law in all states.

Story Time

Mark and Melissa Wandall were nine months pregnant with their daughter Madisyn. They were driving back from dinner with Melissa's brother Phil when a red-light runner crashed into them. Mark died, and Phil was left with horrible injuries that still affect his life to this day. Melissa raised Madisyn all by herself, and while Madisyn is thriving in life, I have no doubt the crash left a huge hole in both their hearts. I can't even imagine going through what Melissa and Madisyn have had to experience over the years. Since then, Melissa became the president of the National Coalition for Safer Roads (NCSR), and through Melissa's passion, commitment, and hard work, she has helped lower the number of injuries and deaths caused by traffic crashes. She was instrumental in passing Florida's Mark Wandall Traffic Safety Act that allows Florida communities to use red light safety cameras to help decrease red-light runners. It doesn't stop there. Melissa is also the founder and president of The Mark Wandall Foundation, a non-profit organization she started in memory of Mark and in honor of Madisyn. The foundation offers resources, programs and assistance to grieving children, teens and young adults. Wow! Through their experience, many wonderful things have come to be. Many lives have no doubt been saved and many drivers have changed their driving behaviors. We need more people like Melissa. She's a HUGE life-changer and difference-maker in this world. She's helping to save lives before we lose them. Feel free to go to the back of the book for more information about Melissa and the work she is doing.

A few tips for traffic lights:

1. Look well down the road to see the upcoming intersection light color.
2. Predict if the light color is going to change by the time you arrive upon it.
3. Glance in your rearview mirror for a quick moment to see who's behind you.
4. Scan left to right as you approach the intersection to see if anyone is going to run their red light.

With over 116,000 injuries at traffic lights in one year—according to the Insurance Institute of Highway Safety—the last thing you'll want to do is run a red light and create a life-changing situation for yourself or others. Be the hero out there on the roads. In the end we are all in this together and need to be responsible and mature. Use your brain, be patient and drive safe. That's a great way to honor Madisyn, Mark, Melissa, and Phil.

55
Trains

Let's talk about trains. Those things are gi-GANTIC!! They are powerful, and nothing stands in their way. According to the Tennessee Department of Safety, the average car weighs about 3,000 pounds, while the average loaded train weighs about 12 million pounds and takes about a mile to stop when it's traveling at 55 miles per hour. So what does that mean? It means that you'll lose every time, so stay out of their way. There are over 700 people killed each year in car/train collisions and thousands injured as well. Trains are a big deal. So you have to respect them and stay out of their way.

Story Time

When I was 18 years old, I was walking to work with my 1980s Walkman on, listening to my favorite tunes. I was running late and decided to take a shortcut and walk on the train tracks across a 300-foot-long bridge. WRONG DECISION. I was about halfway across the bridge when I decided to take a quick glance behind me. Just then, I noticed an Amtrak train approaching the bridge at about 45 miles per hour. I had three options:

1. I could try to outrun the train. Would never work!
2. Jump over the bridge and fall about 30 feet to the concrete sewer below.
3. Die!

No, no, no. Laying down on the tracks wouldn't work, so let's not mention that. I decided to jump over the rail, and sure enough, when they say that your life flashes past you, they weren't kidding. Everything appeared to just go in slow motion, and as I flew over the rail, I reached back and grabbed it as tight as I could and barely held on. The rail was covered with grease that had been released from all the trains over the months and years. I dangled from the rail as the train rushed by with passengers aboard who had no idea that the train they were on almost killed a teen. To this day, I wonder if my stupid decision still affects the train conductor. He has no idea if I jumped over that rail to my death or not.

So what's the big take away? Stay away from the train tracks! What about when you are approaching a red light? Don't stop on train tracks. Stop before or after the tracks, and make sure no part of your car is close enough to the tracks for a train to hit. If you see the railroad crossing lights flashing, don't try to beat the safety arm before it lowers; you're just taking a chance with your life.

A few tips about trains:

1. Don't expect to hear the train's horn. Sometimes traffic noise, your conversation with passengers, your music, etc., blocks out the horn.
2. Pay attention to your driving at all times.
3. Don't shift gears and possibly stall your car when going over tracks. You might get stuck.
3. Many tracks don't have safety arms, but that doesn't mean you have free rein to drive over the tracks. Look in both directions when approaching the tracks.
4. Don't go around the crossing gate when it is down; you could die, dude!
5. Bring your vehicle to a complete stop no closer than fifteen feet before the nearest track.
6. If your vehicle is stuck on the track, and a train is coming, and you don't want to die, then get out of the car as fast as you can and get off the tracks. Once you are off the tracks, run away from your vehicle at a 45-degree angle in the direction of the oncoming train so when the train hits your vehicle, the debris is way behind you at the point of impact. Can you picture that?

Be aware of the vehicles that are required by law to stop at all railroad crossings, such as school buses, passenger buses, and trucks carrying hazardous, flammable, or explosive materials. You must be patient and let them make their full stop and then continue. Don't be a dork and go around them.

As you can guess, I'm extra sensitive decades later when it comes to railroad tracks. I'm much more aware of tracks than the average driver. Many times, when we are rushing to get somewhere, we compromise our driving and make decisions we would not normally make. So slow down, be aware, and arrive safely to your destination.

56
Trust

Your parents love you. They want the best for you. Up to this point, they have been trying to set you up for success. You are very close to getting a license (unless you already have one), and they want to know they can trust you with the car. Don't blow their trust and have to ride the school bus again. When you become a parent, you'll understand more what it's like waiting for your teen to come home on time in one piece. That's what life is like for Brenda and me for our daughters. We want to know that they are where they say they are going to be. If they have an idea of going somewhere else, then we expect them to call us to ask for permission.

    I know of many parents who don't care where their teens are with the car, as long as they are home by curfew. The problem with that is many teens will do things that they KNOW their parents don't approve of. If you spend your time doing the right things, then you won't have the time to do the wrong things. I sound like a broken record saying it yet again, but it's important! Do the right things, and keep the relationship with your family open, honest, and healthy.

Story Time

Two teen guys were out with friends drinking beers. Their parents didn't know. They got a ride home to one of their houses and hung out for a while. The parents were asleep. Then one teen took his dad's $90,000 car and drove his buddy home. After dropping him off, he put the car in a ditch because he was still intoxicated. He had to call his parents at the crash scene, wake them up, and have them come meet him and the police.

Now that is a good example of breaking his parents' trust in him. Are you going to do something that stupid? Perhaps you already have.

A few things to think about when it comes to trust:

1. Don't say you MIGHT do something to give yourself the excuse of changing your mind. Many dopey parents don't pick up on the word "might."
2. Don't tell half-truths. A half-truth is still lying.
3. Take care of the vehicle your parents have blessed you with. It shows maturity and responsibility.
4. Do what you say you are going to do, no matter what it is.
5. Say what you mean and mean what you say.

6. Don't play the "I don't remember" card. If you don't remember things, then how can your parents trust you?

Your parents have invested a lot in you and want the best for you. Perhaps at some point in your early teen years you started developing an independent spirit with your own thoughts, and they didn't line up with what your parents wanted for you. Now you find yourself hiding a lot of stuff from them. Well, that actually can bruise your relationship with them. Sure, they might get mad at you when you break the rules or do stupid things, but it's because they didn't raise you that way. So make your parents proud. Make yourself proud. Keep your self-respect, and do the right, safe, and legal things in life. Don't bow down to any peer pressure, and don't be THAT idiot who influences others in a bad way to break the trust with their own families. Don't be average. Be excellent!

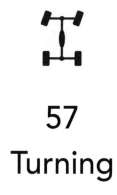

57
Turning

I have a lot to share on this subject, so please soak it all up. A lot of drivers take turning for granted. It appears to be a simple task, but in my years of coaching new drivers, I've come to learn that it really is more mental than people realize. Looking down the road at the upcoming intersection is vital. If you do that, then you'll be able to process how many left, straight, and right turn lanes there are. I've noticed that many new drivers aren't looking down the road enough and don't realize there is even a right turn lane until the last moment, and then they try to get over into it too late. For the most part, turning should be hand-over-hand on the steering wheel. You can always watch videos online about hand-over-hand turning. Make sure you don't oversteer or understeer.

Story Time

Years ago, I was on a lesson with a teen, and we came to a four-way stop intersection. He made his stop and then made a very wide right turn, almost swiping the side of a police car. The cop made a U-turn and pulled us over. He approached our car and jokingly asked our teen driver if he had been drinking. The teen explained that it was his first driving lesson. The cop told him to keep practicing and be careful, and then he sent us on our way. That's the only time I've ever been pulled over while on a driving lesson!

Another Story

Recently I drove on a first lesson with a teen whose parents hardly practiced with her. This sweet girl did the best she could, but she was all over the road. At one point, she attempted a right turn at a corner but didn't straighten her steering wheel after the turn. She kept turning. It's called an oversteer. She could have hit the right curb and run up over it. Because of my superhero fast moves, I was able to grab the steering wheel with my left hand and return it back to straight, only to jam one of my fingers on the steering wheel in the process. I didn't let her know I was in pain for the next hour. I had to ice my finger when I got home and had disrupted sleep from the pain. Fortunately, I have ice in my veins for the most part and am pretty calm and cool. I encouraged her and kept praising her efforts. I was very proud of her for pushing aside her fear and driving almost 35 miles around town with me.

A few tips about turning:
Right turn on red lights

1. Signal about 50-100 feet before entering the right turn lane.

2. Slow down and check your rearview mirror to see who's behind you so you don't get rear-ended.
3. Stop at your stop line to obey the law.
4. Look to your right down the sidewalk for pedestrians.
5. Move forward to get a better glance for oncoming cars from your left.
6. Also, check the other side of the intersection for vehicles with a green left-turn arrow.
7. If the way is clear, then complete your right turn.
8. If the way is not clear, then you might have to stop a second time, but make sure you glance in your rearview mirror again, because sometimes the driver behind you is looking to their left as well and could rear-end your back bumper.

Left turn at green lights

1. Hopefully, you'll have a green arrow, but if it's a green light, then you can stay behind the stop line and wait for oncoming traffic to clear, or you can move into the intersection and wait. It depends on the laws in your area.
2. Keep your wheels pointed straight in case you get rear-ended.
3. Glance in your rearview mirror to see if anyone is waiting behind you.
4. Don't assume oncoming traffic will stop on their yellow or red light.

5. Remember, you have to give the right-of-way to cars going straight and turning right.//
6. Make a 90-degree turn into your correct lane.
7. You may complete it on a red light, because that's not considered running a red light. It's finishing on a red light.
8. Make sure you turn into the correct lane according to any arrows posted.
9. After completing your turn, make sure to check your rearview mirror to see if any cars are flying up on your rear.

Those are a lot of tips, but they are very important. Just keep practicing, and you'll do really well. Go out with your family and practice making right and left turns, and don't come back to your house until you've completed twenty or thirty. Set a number, and make it happen. Practice makes progress.

Acknowledgements

Thank you to Ashley Hagan, an amazing editor and fun person to bounce my crazy thoughts off of – and for making my "write like I speak" read better than I actually do speak. I hope you had as much fun as I did with this project.

Thank you Brian Gall. Your phenomenal talent for creating the cover art is top notch. You rock!

Thank you Brian Kannard for your awesome page design and cover design!

Thank you very much to my wife Brenda Da Babe for your patience and encouragement during the writing process.

Thank you to my three daughters: Isabella, Daniella and Alexa. It was wonderful taking you all through the driving process. We had a lot of laughs and good daddy/daughter time. I'm proud of the safe drivers you have become and extra proud that you see the big picture that we are all in this together trying to get around safely.

Thank you to all the parents who've trusted me in coaching and teaching your teens to be the safest, defensive drivers possible. All of us working together can make the roads safer.

Thank you to all the teens over the decades for being teachable and coachable. You help me be a better Driving Coach and motivate me to continue learning so I can pass critical driving knowledge on to you. **I like biscuits!**

Resources

Spanky's Driving Academy: spankysdrivingacademy.com

Youtube: youtube.com/user/SpankysDriving

Facebook: facebook.com/spankysdriving

National Highway Transportation Safety Administration: nhtsa.gov

AAA: aaa.com

Governors Highway Safety Association: ghsa.org

The Mark Wandall Foundation: themarkwandallfoundation.org

National Coalition for Safer Roads: ncsrsafety.org

Insurance Institute of Highway Safety: Iihs.org

School Bus Fleet: schoolbusfleet.com

National Association of State Directors of Pupil Transportation Services: nasdpts.org

Made in the USA
Columbia, SC
02 June 2024

36299280R00115